Fort Toulouse

The Library of Alabama Classics,
reprint editions of works important
to the history, literature, and culture of
Alabama, is dedicated to the memory of
Rucker Agee
whose pioneering work in the fields
of Alabama history and historical geography
continues to be the standard of
scholarly achievement.

Fort Toulouse
The French Outpost at the Alabamas on the Coosa

Daniel H. Thomas

with an Introduction by
Gregory A. Waselkov

The University of Alabama Press
Tuscaloosa

"Fort Toulouse: The French Outpost at the Alabamas
on the Coosa," by Daniel H. Thomas, is published
courtesy of Alabama State Department of Archives
and History. It appeared originally in the Fall
1960 issue of *The Alabama Historical Quarterly*,
published by the Alabama State Department of Archives
and History.

Library of Congress Cataloging-in-Publication Data

Thomas, Daniel H.
  Fort Toulouse : the French outpost at the Alabamas on the Coosa/
by Daniel H. Thomas; with an introduction by Gregory Waselkov.
      p.   cm.—(The Library of Alabama classics)
  "Appeared originally in the Fall 1960 issue of the Alabama
historical quarterly"—T.p. verso.
  Bibliography: p.
  ISBN 0-8173-0421-5 (pbk. : alk. paper)
  ISBN 978-0-8173-0421-8
  ISBN 978-0-8173-8478-4 (electronic)

  1. Fort Toulouse Site (Ala.)   2. French—Alabama—History—18th
century.   3. Alabama—History—To 1819.   4. Wetumpka Region (Ala.)—
Antiquities.   5. Alabama—Antiquities.   I. Title.   II. Series.
F334.F76T46   1989
976.1'52—dc19
                                                      88-17529

CONTENTS

Artifacts excavated from Fort Toulouse II (1751–1763) and contemporaneous Indian village sites. Back: brass kettle, French lead glazed redware bowl, pewter or latten spoon; Middle: English white clay pipe, French wine bottle, Bohemian engraved glass tumbler (probably French); Front: French Faience plate, iron fork with two-piece bone handle. (Courtesy of the Alabama Historical Commission and the Alabama Department of Archives and History; Photograph by Paula Weiss).

INTRODUCTION:
Recent Archaeological and Historical Research

Gregory A. Waselkov

To the French, Fort Toulouse was simply, but emphatically, "the key to the country." The English, who found their plans for economic and political control of the Southeast so often thwarted there, called it the "mischievous French garrison *Alebámah.*" And the Creek Indians, with their genius for self-determination amid the conflicting demands of powerful colonial neighbors, knew it as "Franca Choka Chula, or the old French trading house."[1] How a small, isolated, poorly supplied outpost played such a significant and varied role in the history of the colonial Southeast has been masterfully explored in this brief volume by Daniel H. Thomas.

The author spent his childhood in the town of Wetumpka, Alabama, just a few miles from the site of the fort, which was a favorite fishing spot for local boys. In 1912 his father officiated at the unveiling of a stone historical marker placed at the site. When he later attended the University of Alabama at Tuscaloosa, Thomas pursued his early interest and selected Fort Toulouse as a topic for a master's thesis, which he completed in 1929. Thomas P. Abernethy, a student of Frederick Jackson Turner and the author of *The Formative Period in Alabama, 1815–1828*, directed Thomas's thesis.

This was an era of remarkable productivity for students of the French colony of Louisiana. In 1918 the *Louisiana Historical Quarterly* began a detailed calendar, in English, of the Superior Council of Louisiana judicial records dating from 1715 to 1763, which was followed by three translated volumes of the *Mississippi Provincial Archives, French Dominion*, published by the Mississippi Department of Archives and History between 1927 and 1932. Except for the still-unsurpassed work of Nancy Miller Surrey on *The Commerce of Louisiana During the French Regime, 1699–1763* (published in 1916), however, few syntheses were attempted that built on the earlier efforts of Peter Hamilton and Charles Gayarré;[2] and certainly nothing appeared to complement Verner Crane's 1928 classic, *The Southern Frontier*, with its primarily British perspective.

Daniel Thomas's narrative history of Fort Toulouse was a modest attempt at synthesis at the local level. But the thesis remained unpublished for over three decades. Meanwhile, the author specialized in modern European diplomatic history,[3] and eventually became chairman of the department of history at the University of Rhode Island. In the late 1950s,

Thomas began a thorough rewriting of his long-neglected thesis. The resulting manuscript comprised the entire fall issue of *The Alabama Historical Quarterly* for 1960.

In addition to incorporating much relevant information from books and articles published in the intervening thirty-one years, Thomas also relied extensively on numerous French manuscript sources. The high standard of scholarship evident in the endnote references largely accounts for the continuing value of Thomas's monograph. With few exceptions, Thomas's conclusions are still valid. Recent advances in our knowledge of Fort Toulouse have resulted mainly from the ongoing program of archaeological excavations at the old fort site and serve to supplement and clarify, rather than correct, the historical scenario first sketched in the book. Thomas did not have an opportunity to proofread his history before publication in 1960; consequently, some typographic errors and the lack of diacritical marks have not been corrected in this facsimile reprint edition. Readers not previously acquainted with Daniel Thomas's book may wish to skip to it now and then return to finish the remainder of the introduction, which reviews new developments and discoveries.

•

Archaeological research at the Fort Toulouse site began in 1972 and continued through 1980, with additional excavations occurring from 1984 to 1986.[4] During the course of this work, numerous artifacts have been found that predate the French occupation of the peninsula. The oldest objects are 8000-year-old projectile points—stone spearheads with corner-notched bases characteristic of the period labeled Early Archaic by archaeologists. Evidently this high bluff between the Coosa and Tallapoosa rivers was repeatedly utilized as a campsite by Archaic hunters and their families. Beginning about 3000 years ago, coinciding with the introduction of pottery to the region, Indian settlements became more permanent. By around A.D. 700, large Late Woodland villages existed to the west and southeast of what would become the fort site.

Sometime after A.D. 1200, a palisaded Mississippian town with at least one ceremonial earthen mound was built immediately west of the future fort location. Although this village seems to have been abandoned by 1540, when de Soto's Spanish army marched down the Coosa River valley, the place was reoccupied in the seventeenth century by refugees from the north, south, and west, the ancestors of central Alabama's historic Indians. The unusual custom of these people to bury their dead in large cooking pots created much interest among archaeologists early in the twentieth century. Consequently, the village site was intensively excavated by members of the Alabama Anthropological Society between

1928 and 1945, and many of their finds are now displayed at the Alabama Department of Archives and History museum in Montgomery.

Perhaps more important than the mode of burial of these protohistoric Indians is the large quantity and variety of trade goods that they managed to obtain from the Spanish missions of Florida. The southeastern Indians had developed and maintained an intricate exchange network by which means marine shells, such as whelks and marginellas, had been traded far inland for centuries before the arrival of the Spaniards. With the establishment of Franciscan missions in northern Florida, new and exotic ornaments entered the network. Such items as glass beads and brass armbands and gorgets moved northward, passed along from village to village, often being exchanged for deerskins sought after by the Spaniards. Trading paths also provided avenues for the spread of Old World contagious diseases, such as smallpox, influenza, and measles, which decimated previously unexposed Indian populations.

When English traders from Charleston first reached the forks of the Coosa and Tallapoosa, perhaps slightly before 1690, they found the Alabama Indians already familiar with European products and ready to open another, larger market for their deerskins. Although the English later claimed to have had a trading warehouse, or factory, among the Alabamas by 1687,[5] it is known for certain only that the Alabamas had close economic ties with English traders in their villages. By the time French colonists founded Mobile in 1702, the Alabamas were actively raiding small coastal tribes to obtain captives for sale to English slave traders. The French soon found themselves unwittingly involved in a war with the English-supplied Alabamas, a conflict that continued until trade abuses finally caused a rift between the English and their Indian allies.[6]

General discontent with the English throughout the Southeast eventually provoked a large-scale uprising, the Yamasee War of 1715. After all of the English traders living in the Alabama towns either had been killed or had fled, the Indians sought other means of obtaining the muskets, ammunition, and other foreign goods upon which they had come to depend. At this critical juncture, the Alabamas devised a strategy that would serve them well for nearly half a century in their dealings with Europeans. A recent amalgam of refugee villages themselves, the Alabamas had previously forged a confederacy with neighboring Muskogee-speaking tribes. This loosely unified polity, known to the English as the Creeks, managed to maintain peace among the many different ethnic groups forming the confederacy while simultaneously tolerating opposing political factions. These factions might support relations with different European powers, but they were all expected to compromise on important issues requiring a general consensus within the tribe or confederacy. The existence of these counterpoised factions led the Creeks to practice neutrality in their dealings with Europeans.[7] As Lieutenant François Hazeur reported from the Alabamas in 1740, "they had long held as a maxim not to meddle at all in the quarrels that the Europeans had among themselves; that they had profited by it, since by means of this policy they were well received by all and received benefits from all sides."[8]

Brims, the "Emperor" of Coweta, a Lower Creek town, reputedly had masterminded this strategy, but its success depended on the existence of a viable alternative to English trade. Thus, the headman known to us only as the Grand Chief of the Alabamas proposed that the French at Mobile build a fort in his village and at his expense.[9] The French neither usurped nor encroached upon the English, as the latter frequently claimed;[10] rather, the developments of 1717 in the Alabama country were due to a coinciding of French design and Indian opportunity.

•

Theophilus Hastings and John Musgrove, the leaders of the English party that unsuccessfully challenged Lieutenant de La Tour's expedition to the Alabamas, were not the only unwelcome visitors to appear at the newly erected fort. In September, 1718, Diego de Peña arrived with orders from the governor of Spanish Florida to derive some advantage from the political and economic vacuum created by the English expulsion from the interior Southeast during the Yamasee War. Peña was at first well received by the officer in command at Fort Toulouse, an unnamed Biscayan, perhaps Lieutenant de La Tour.[11] The Biscayan even showed Peña some pieces of rock, supposed to contain silver, that he had found nearby. Presumably the Frenchman had obtained this "ore" from a place labeled on contemporary maps as "Mines de la Tour," located about 200 miles by boat up the Alabama River from Mobile.[12] The rock may have been a metamorphic stone, perhaps the silvery-looking micaceous schists sometimes found in gravel beds in this region.

Soon afterward, three large boats arrived carrying an officer to relieve the Biscayan, "a great quantity of goods, his woman, and ten Frenchmen." The new commandant, who was less hospitable than his predecessor had been to the strange Spaniard lingering about this distant outpost, bluntly told Peña that he should leave immediately and would be arrested if he returned.[13] The Spaniards never posed a serious threat to the French at Fort Toulouse, but this incident does serve to illustrate the three-sided nature of the contest for colonial influence in the region.

•

The precise, original location of Fort Toulouse remained unknown until 1986, when an excavation team from the University of Alabama investigated a narrow strip of land along the bank of the Coosa River.[14] Discovered here were a portion of a deep moat and footing trenches for a corner bastion and one curtain palisade (Figure 1). Less than one quarter of the fort site has survived the inexorable erosive force of the Coosa in flood, the very cause of the structure's abandonment in 1751. This first fort, which is now referred to as Fort Toulouse I, probably measured about 150 feet between furthermost bastion points.[15] La Tour's original design undoubtedly was smaller, since the French enlarged the fort in 1735.[16]

The dry moat may have been added in 1725 during an effort to repair and strengthen the fort. A 1747 documentary reference to the moat describes it as "a Ditch 12 Feet deep," something of an exaggeration judging from the excavated dimensions of 15½ feet wide by 7½ feet deep.[17]

More still may be learned about the physical appearance of Fort Toulouse I when archaeologists return to excavate the remaining unexplored area of the fort interior.

•

With the French firmly ensconced among the Alabamas, the English attempted to persuade the Indians that they, too, needed a fort in the

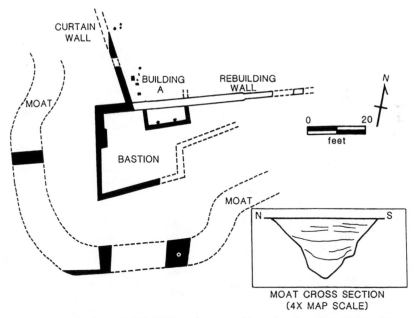

Figure 1. Fort Toulouse I (1717–1751), as determined by archaeological excavations (Courtesy of Richard Krause, University of Alabama, and Ned Jenkins, Alabama Historical Commission).

Creek country. As early as 1727, the South Carolinians requested permission to build a fort at Okfuskee town, so that traders could take refuge there during times of trouble.[18] The Creeks, however, consistently refused to allow a fort to be built at Okfuskee or elsewhere until the establishment of the new English colony of Georgia altered the political status quo in the region. The Georgians claimed jurisdiction over traders operating among the Creeks, and they sought to exclude South Carolinians from the trade. To enforce this restriction, Governor Oglethorpe dispatched Patrick McKay in 1735 to expel unlicensed traders and negotiate with the Creeks. McKay demanded that the Creeks demolish the French fort at the Alabamas. If they refused, then he should be allowed to build a fort of his own, or, McKay threatened, he would withdraw all traders. Faced with this ultimatum, Creek leaders felt they could not risk a break in trade relations with either the French or the English. After a week-long deliberation, their council reluctantly consented to allow McKay to build a fort at a site of his choosing.[19]

Despite French protests, by late 1736 Lieutenant Anthony Willey arrived at Okfuskee, where he was "stationed at a small Fort, with two or three Men."[20] There they remained, enforcing trade regulations, until 1742, when Captain Richard Kent, senior ranger officer in Georgia, took command. Kent and his three-man garrison apparently abandoned the post sometime the following year.[21]

With this lapse the South Carolinians reasserted their interest in establishing a fort among the Creeks. Across the Tallapoosa River from Okfuskee, the trader Alexander Wood and the pro-English faction of that town erected "a Palisade Fort 150 Feet Square" near the traders' storehouses.[22] They finished the task in March, 1744, but the South Carolina Commons House of Assembly balked at the expense of garrisoning such a remote outpost.

> It is impracticable to carry Cannon thither for the Defence of
> a Garrison, or to supply it with Provisions, or to give it any
> timely or effectual Relief, the Distance being so great . . .
> we apprehend the sole Design of building that Fort was for
> the Traders to retreat to while the Indians were out a hunt-
> ing, that they might be there in a Body together, and con-
> sequently better able to defend themselves against any
> Attempt of the Alabama Garrison.[23]

By October, 1745, Governor Vaudreuil of Louisiana had ascertained that:

> the so-called fort of the Great Akfaské, which was less a fort
> than anything, has totally fallen into ruins of itself. It was only

> a house surrounded by a stockade, which was occupied by the
> English traders [and] which they seem to have abandoned
> since then. . . .[24]

The French commandants at Fort Toulouse had worked assiduously to
undermine English support at Okfuskee by supplying presents, including
good quality muskets, to leaders of the pro-French faction. With no military assistance forthcoming from South Carolina and the situation among
the Creeks deteriorating, Wood and his fellow traders dropped their attempt to reestablish an English fort in the Creek country.

Both forts at Okfuskee had been small structures, but the Georgia fort,
at least, with its token garrison, had been a significant attempt to establish
an official English presence. Lieutenant Willey had tried to impose some
order on the unruly traders, who frequently jeopardized English diplomatic policy toward the Indians for private economic gain.[25] Final abandonment of the Okfuskee post left the traders virtually unregulated, a
situation that undoubtedly contributed to the disaffection of many Creeks
and enhanced the influence of the French at Fort Toulouse.

•

By 1748 the dilapidated state of Fort Toulouse prompted Governor
Vaudreuil to dispatch sub-engineer François Saucier for an inspection.
Saucier's construction diagrams for the fort completed three years later
have never been found. But recent archaeological work, particulary the
1984 excavations by archaeologists from Auburn University at Montgomery, has revealed nearly the entire plan of Fort Toulouse II (Figure 2).[26]
The new fort was located about 100 feet south of the older structure.

Excavation of the Fort Toulouse II palisade trench uncovered the bases
of timbers that had been quartered and charred, then set upright in a
trench nearly 3 feet deep (Figure 3). The charring was an attempt to make
the posts resistant to rot and insect damage, serious concerns in the
warm, moist climate of the region. Behind these were smaller, uncharred
support posts that closed some of the gaps left between the main palisade
posts.[27] Charcoal samples from nine charred posts have been identified as
three specimens each of pine (*Pinus* sp.), oak or chestnut (*Quercus* sp. or
Castanea sp.), and birch (Family Betulaceae).[28] Construction details de-
duced from the archaeological remains coincide closely with instructions
issued in 1734 for repairs to the stockade of Fort Toulouse I. These specified "oak piles three feet in circumference, without bark, by nine feet
high of which the lower part that is to be placed in the ground shall be
charred, all well trimmed and nailed. . . ."[29] Instructions sent to other

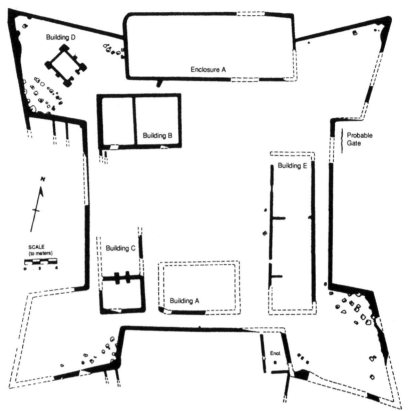

Figure 2. Fort Toulouse II (1751–1763), as determined by archaeological excavations.

forts called for the "piles" to be quartered and reinforced on the palisade interior with shorter posts, all nailed to horizontal laths.[30]

The fort outline is not symmetrical, since various segments of the palisade differ in length. Curtains, the walls between bastions, range from 65½ – 69 feet in length, and the distance from bastion point to point is 152½ – 157½ feet. Bastion faces measure 38½ – 49 feet and bastion flanks from 11½ – 24 feet long. The total extrapolated palisade length is 797 feet, with an average of about 26 main uprights and 18 support posts per 10 feet of palisade. The charred posts were split from logs originally 1 to 1½ feet in diameter, so about 500 logs of this size would have been sufficient to build the palisade, with an additional 1500 boards and posts of different widths (ranging from 2 to 12 inches) for the supports and laths.

Each main palisade post undoubtedly was sharpened to a point at the top. In 1756, the garrison was said to "have put iron Spikes on the Heads of the Puncheons" as an additional precaution against attack.[31]

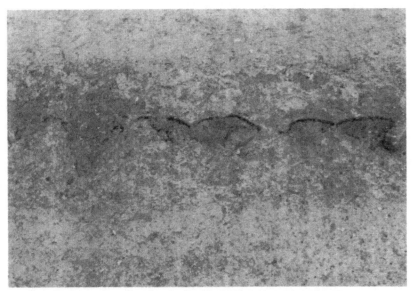

Figure 3. Charred, quartered posts in palisade trench, Fort Toulouse II.

Figure 4. Footing trench of Building D, the powder magazine of Fort Toulouse II.

Saucier's fort outline generally conforms to the classic Vauban pattern of fortification construction, with corner bastions designed to provide enfilading fire covering the curtains. However, there are some features that suggest defensibility was not an overriding concern of those in command. One eccentricity in the fort plan is the large palisaded enclosure (see Enclosure A in Figure 2), between the two northern bastions. The enclosure trench contains charred, quartered posts identical to those found elsewhere in the palisade trenches. Encompassing an area 67 by 26 feet in extent, Enclosure A seems to have been added to the completed fort palisade as an afterthought, as can be seen by the discontinuous post patterns excavated at the bastion flank/enclosure wall junctions. What purpose this enclosure served remains a mystery, but a similar picketed enclosure is depicted on a map of the Spanish fort at Pensacola in 1720, where a colonial official had fenced the area outside a curtain between two bastions for his garden.[32] Enclosure A is situated adjacent to the steep Coosa River bluff, the side of the fort considered least vulnerable to attack. Perhaps construction of Enclosure A was simply an expedient way to expand the cramped confines of the fort—for a livestock pen, a garden, or some other purpose—even though it violated a basic tenet of military engineering.

A gate probably existed in the east curtain near the northeast bastion. Unfortunately, most of this portion of the palisade was destroyed in 1814 during construction of Fort Jackson, an American fort built on the same site as Fort Toulouse II. But evidence from the remaining portion of wall trench suggests that there was a gap in the palisade 6 feet wide at this spot.

No evidence of catwalks exists along any of the curtains. Presumably, the garrison could have fired through loopholes or gaps in the palisade above the secondary support posts. At the points of several bastions a few postholes were found, which indicate that small triangular platforms were placed there, perhaps for sentry boxes.

Within every bastion were two larger platforms, one at each side (in what are called the flanking angles). All of these very probably served as combination sentry/cannon platforms. Archaeological evidence consists of one to three rows of square postholes, each of which contains a round, uncharred postmold about 8 inches in diameter. These posts would have supported sleepers that abutted the interior flanking angle walls and were floored with hewn planks. Within each bastion, one platform measured about 6 feet deep and 10 feet wide, and the other was pentagonal in shape, 13 feet deep and 16½ feet wide. The larger platforms could have supported artillery pieces protecting the adjoining curtains. These sorts of sentry and gun platforms were common features of French forts in North America.[33] A description of Fort Ascension, on the lower Ohio River, in

1758 mentions "platforms placed at the flanked angles of the bastions for placing the *guerrites* [circular sentry boxes] and some cannon. . . ."[34]

Five structures within the fort have been excavated since 1979.[35] Building A is known only from a 12-foot length of wall trench. It is thought to be similar to Building B, which was a two-room structure, measuring 21⅓ by 32¾ feet. Buildings C and E were also paired structures facing each other across the parade ground; they may have served as rowhouse-style barracks. Each was about 63 feet long by 17 ½ feet wide. Building interiors were divided by two partition walls into three rooms, all of which were heated by H-shaped brick fireplaces in the partitions. Two or three doors existed on the parade-ground sides of each building. In a case of remarkable archaeological preservation, the remains of one of the Building C doors was discovered in 1985; it measured 2 feet wide by just 4½ feet tall and originally stood on a brick sill.[36] The absence of drip lines (caused by rain running off the eaves of the roof) outside any of the walls indicates that the buildings lacked porches or galleries.

The fifth structure (Building D) located in the fort interior was a small building (8 feet 9 inches by 11 feet 7 inches) situated in the center of the northwest bastion (Figure 4). The wall footing trenches, which had been dug very neatly, held widely spaced, vertical wall posts set 28 inches into the ground. Outside the main trenches were additional footings for buttress posts placed 20 inches deep. The structure is thought to have been the fort's powder magazine, based on analogy with other French forts in North America. Time and again the French chose to locate powder magazines in bastions, at Fort Maurepas (1699), New Biloxi (1721), and Fort Condé (1724).[37] Even more significant, perhaps, are the size and construction technique, both of which reflect building function. A powder magazine was typically one of the smallest, but also one of the most substantial, buildings within any fort. At Fort Maurepas, for instance, the wooden magazine's side walls supported an arched roof; the floor sills rested on piers and the sides were propped with short buttresses. Vaulted powder magazines also were built at La Balise, Fort Tombecbé, Fort Michilimackinac, and at Fort de Chartres, which was designed by the same François Saucier who planned and built Fort Toulouse II.[38] Most of these structures were covered with earth and sod for protection from fire and enemy artillery, but the Fort Tombecbé magazine was roofed with shingles.[39] So the precise appearance of Building D at Fort Toulouse II remains conjectural, though the function seems well established.[40]

The French in Louisiana employed two principal methods for constructing wooden buildings. *Pieux en terre* or *poteaux en terre* (post-in-ground) used posts set close together in trenches to form the walls. Since the wall posts were placed directly in the footing trench, such houses usually succumbed to rot and termite damage rather quickly; one example, however, dating from the 1720s still stands in Pascagoula, Mississippi.[41] A description of such a house, written at Kaskaskia in 1758, indicates the simple nature of these structures; "One house built of pickets well plastered, covered with shingles, with a stone chimney, a shed on one side. . . ."[42]

Poteaux sur sole (post-on-sill), the other building method, involved mortising wall uprights into horizontal wooden sills. The sills often were raised on stone or wooden piers, and the result was a somewhat more elaborate structure, as exemplified by this description from New Chartres in 1760:

> One house built on sills, covered with shingles, consisting of one room, and two small closets and one shed, the room and one closet floored above and below, with mud partition wall, one stone chimney. . . .[43]

In both types of house, the spaces between upright posts were filled with *colombage*, a general term referring either to *bousillage* (mud, mixed with grass or Spanish moss, plastered over wooden slats or laths) or to *pierrotage* (mortar and stones).[44]

Only Building E, one of the long barracks at Fort Toulouse, appears to have been a *pieux en terre* structure. Evidence of closely spaced posts was found in the bottom of the wall trenches. The upper levels of the Building E trenches, however, contained just a few, widely spaced postholes. Apparently, Building E was originally constructed using the *pieux en terre* method, and may even predate the rest of the fort. Later, presumably because the wall posts were decaying (as the presence of postmolds deep in the trenches indicates), the building was dismantled and reconstructed using a variation of the *poteaux sur sole* technique.

All five structures in Fort Toulouse II, including the rebuilt Building E, have two features in common: (1) continuous wall trenches, and (2) widely spaced, square postholes, many of which are filled with a gray clay closely resembling Creek Indian potters' clay. From its location in postholes, however, the clay is thought actually to be *bousillage* that had filtered gradually into the holes as the buildings decayed after abandonment. This further suggests that the posts set in these holes were the main structural uprights, which were usually set on sills in *poteaux sur sole* construction. Short sections of horizontal sills were probably laid in the footing trenches and mortised to the uprights, instead of being raised on piers, and could have supported floor joists. An identical construction method was used to build a Jesuit mission at Cahokia in 1735, and elsewhere the French are known to have employed structure foundations of squared timbers laid in trenches.[45]

Bricks and brick fragments were some of the most common artifacts found during the Fort Toulouse excavations, but their use seems to have been limited to fireplaces and door sills. A chemical analysis of the bricks and the local clay subsoil indicates that the bricks were very probably made at the fort.[46] Certainly the bricks differ in size and appearance from those found at French-period sites in Mobile.[47] Furthermore, the laborious upstream water carriage could barely supply the fort with essential provisions and trade goods; bricks must have been a low priority, indeed, for the bateaux crews. The bricks were made in individual wooden forms. After the forms were wetted and some sand tossed inside, moist clay was pressed in and the excess scraped off. This was the common mode of brick manufacture throughout the eighteenth century and produced bricks with one striated and five sandy surfaces.[48] After they had been sun-dried, the bricks would then have been stacked to form a kiln. Those bricks that were closest to the center, and consequently nearest the fire, have one or more glazed surfaces.

Various sorts of small ancillary structures must have existed within or near the fort, although none have been identified in the excavated area. One might expect eventually to find ovens, latrines, and a well. Dome-shaped French ovens made of clay and sticks sat on raised platforms under shed roofs.[49] Wells in French Illinois in the 1720s had wood and *bousillage* boxes at least 2½ feet high, shingle-covered shed roofs, and ropes and pulleys for drawing water.[50] Of course, empty barrels could have been used to catch rainwater from houses with gutters.[51]

•

The garrison at Fort Toulouse gradually accumulated an impressive complement of artillery for a frontier outpost. In 1720, an English spy reported "3 or 4 small swivel guns" in their possession.[52] By 1732, there were "2 cannons, 2 cast-iron and 2 iron *pierriers*, and 7 *pierrier* breech-blocks."[53] A *pierrier* was a lightweight cannon with removable breech-block, typically mounted as a swivel gun.[54] Still later, Edmond Atkin wrote of the fort as

> . . . having only two Carriage Guns and four Swivel Guns; 'til
> being alarmed with our Intentions to attack it the beginning
> of 1747, the French reinforced it to 45 Men, with two pieces
> of Cannon more, and otherways strengthened it.[55]

These two new pieces of armament were described by Governor Vaudreuil as "a small cannon and a *pierrier*."[56] The last reference, again by an English spy, states that the Alabama garrison in 1756 had "a few

Guns of no heavy Mettal, the particular Number I have not been able to come at."[57] These cannons saw service only as signal and salute guns, primarily upon arrival of a supply bateau from Mobile or during visits by Indian leaders.[58]

After the French abandonment of the fort in 1763, several travelers mentioned seeing cannons lying about the site. In 1777, William Bartram noted "half buried in the earth, a few pieces of ordnance, four and six pounders."[59] Twenty years later, Benjamin Hawkins described the same scene. "In the yard of the town house [at the Alabama town of Taskigi] are five cannons of iron, with the trunnions broke off. . . ."[60]

Archaeological evidence provides some additional information on the types of cannons mounted on the gun platforms of Fort Toulouse II. A cannon barrel with its breech blown off, now in the collections of the Alabama Department of Archives and History, is reputed to be from Fort Toulouse.[61] Although a precise measurement is not possible due to surface corrosion, the piece has a bore diameter of about 3⅓ inches, which is approximately equivalent to the caliber of a French four-pounder.[62] Two broken, iron cannon trunnions (the projections at the middle of the barrel upon which a cannon pivots) have been found with cross section diameters of 2½ and 2²¹⁄₃₂ inches.[63] As a rule, a trunnion's diameter is roughly equal to the diameter of the shot for any particular swivel or carriage gun, so the two excavated examples probably come from French two-pounders of 2.631 caliber.[64] The small size of these trunnions suggests that the guns were swivel-mounted. Finally, five cannonballs have been recovered from archaeological features: one fragmentary six-pound ball, and four complete cast-iron balls ranging in diameter from 2½ to 3⅛ inches and weighing 1.3 to 1.7 pounds (1.24 to 1.59 French *livres*).[65]

When all evidence is considered, the majority of Fort Toulouse artillery seems to have been one- and two-pounder brass and iron swivel guns, with some lesser number of iron four- and six-pounder carriage guns. Some of the latter may have been mounted on field carriages in the parade ground, as was the case at Fort Tombecbé in 1763.[66] But most undoubtedly were mounted on garrison carriages for use on the gun platforms. Mid-eighteenth-century French garrison carriages resembled naval carriages, but had short trails and two front wheels, or trucks, made of cast iron. Normal height of garrison mounted guns was 26 inches above the platform, which sloped about 7½ inches toward the parapet.[67] Embrasures were probably cut through the palisade for the larger guns, but swivels could have been mounted directly on the palisade uprights.[68] Even though the French never had to rely on these guns for defense, the presence of artillery at Fort Toulouse undoubtedly deterred any plans the English had to attack the post.

•

The French military dominated life at the Alabama post. However, as ex-soldiers stayed on after their terms of enlistment had expired and turned to farming, and as other colonists decided to settle around the fort, a considerable civilian community evolved. By 1755, according to an English estimate, "the Number of Men, Women and Children in and about the Albamah Fort consisted of about one Hundred and forty," including 40 soldiers.[69] Unfortunately, the church records of the Capuchin and Jesuit missions to the Alabama post have been lost, and only one detailed post census still exists.[70] But much can still be learned about the French population at Fort Toulouse from monthly garrison lists, especially for the period 1756 to 1763, and the marriage, baptismal, and burial records for Mobile parish.[71] A total of 268 named individuals (91 private soldiers, 44 officers, 58 other men, 39 women, and 36 infants), who are known to have lived for some time at the post, have been identified.[72] This sample, gleaned from archival sources, provides some insights into a colonial settlement long neglected by historians.

Changes in garrison size can be determined fairly precisely. About 20 to 30 soldiers were stationed at the fort between 1717 and 1721, the year when two-thirds of the men mutinied and were either killed or recaptured and imprisoned. The depleted garrison remained small for the next several decades, until reinforced to 50 men by 1751. Because occasional desertions continued to take a toll after 1751, garrison size fluctuated around 40 until the end of the fort's occupation in 1763.

Estimating total post population through time is much more difficult. Apart from the garrison, the only other inhabitants during the first few years were several traders living with the Alabama Indians. A census enumerates 13 men in 1721; however, columns for women, children, French servants, and Indian and Negro slaves were left blank. From this point the population gradually rose to 94 in 1741 and to 140 individuals (including about 80 born there) by 1755.[73] The average annual growth rate between 1721 and 1755 was 3.4 percent, a figure comparable to the growth rates in most of England's North American colonies.[74]

Although information is sparse, there seem to have been many more men than women in this village throughout its history—a characteristic typical of colonizing outposts. The first French woman at the fort, as far as we know, was Marie La Sueur, who married Lieutenant de La Tour in 1720, but stayed only a few months at the fort.[75] In the next 15 years, at least a dozen women came to the fort to be married, and many remained to raise families. Of course, some untold number of French men found Indian wives and mistresses in the Alabama villages located nearby. Father La Vente, the Mobile parish priest, expressed the view of many when he wrote in 1708, "we do not see that the blood of the Indians can do any harm to the blood of the French. . . ."[76] Louis XV disagreed and forbade marriage with native women in 1728.[77] Captain Marchand may have, as legend has it, married the Creek woman, Sehoy, at the fort in 1721, but succeeding commandants did not follow his example.[78] When Jean Charles Trouillet, the storehouse keeper at the fort, had his three-month-old daughter baptized in 1750, he acknowledged a liaison with his female Indian slave; few of his contemporaries were so forthright.[79]

Garrison lists from the 1750s and 1760s indicate a relatively stable community. Of the 40 soldiers present in 1758, 26 (65 percent) were still at the post in 1763, one had died, and at least three had been reassigned. Many of those who remained were related members of extended families descended from two soldiers of the 1721 garrison: Simon Brignac (four descendants) and Pierre Fonteneau (seven descendants). The Creole offspring of these two patriarchs were linked by marriages in 1747, 1756, and 1760.[80]

The ages at which Alabama post inhabitants married is known for seven couples: women ranged in age from 13 to 25 (averaging 18 years); men married between 22 and 30 (most frequently around 28 years of age). While a generalization from this tiny sample would be risky, a much larger sample from Natchitoches Post between 1729 and 1757 also shows a pattern of early female and delayed male marriage.[81] Marriage tended to occur in midwinter or, more frequently, in the spring.[82] In France, weddings usually took place in midwinter, after a family's pigs had been butchered and the stored meat was available for wedding feasts.[83] At Fort Toulouse, where priests were stationed infrequently, those individuals wishing to marry would often have had to go to Mobile, and the principal means of travel was in the bateaux that went down river during high water in the spring.[84]

Births tended to occur mainly in winter and spring. Late summer and fall were times of high mortality, perhaps due to the prevalence of fevers at that season.

Other aspects of the population structure at Fort Toulouse, such as the average age at death, the number of children per family, and the average household composition are beyond our grasp with the scant available data. We know only that two soldiers died in their twenties, that the married women had as many as eleven children (but that three was more common), and that there was at least one black slave there in 1743, and a few Indian slaves throughout the occupation of the village.

•

Artifacts, the broken and discarded material possessions of the Alabama post inhabitants, are frequently more informative concerning daily life than are contemporary documents, most of which are official reports writ-ten for the colonial minister in France. Estate inventories compiled upon the death of a head of household must have once existed, but all now are lost.[85] Since archaeological excavations have focused on Fort Toulouse II, few artifacts have been recovered from the period preceding 1751. At first, household furnishings must have been simple, commonly including a table with straight-backed chairs, a clothes chest or two, a box bed with a straw mattress, wool blankets, wooden plates, perhaps a few pieces of red-glazed or green-glazed earthenware, and brass and iron kettles hang-ing from a pothook in the fireplace.[86] Later the variety of objects in-creased considerably, but conditions always remained spartan in comparison to life in Mobile or New Orleans.

For instance, windows in the second fort's structures were shuttered since glass was unavailable. The lock to an armoir, a French-style ward-robe probably belonging to an officer, has been found, but such a large piece of furniture must have been very unusual. The villagers could have made wood-splint baskets themselves, or traded for Indian-made, split cane baskets.[87]

The Alabama Indians also provided many of the ceramic vessels, mostly storage types, needed in the village and even copied some French and Spanish forms.[88] By the 1750s, sufficient quantities of French-made ce-ramics were being supplied to the post for all households to have faience plates and platters (see frontispiece).[89] Much of this imported ware came from La Rochelle and Rouen, the preeminent ports for colonial trade.[90]

Presumably most clothing also came from France, although the only di-rect evidence is in the form of metal buttons, buckles, and braid. Habi-tants, as the civilian men were known, generally wore loose shirts of cotton or wool, knee breeches, wool stockings, leather shoes—wooden shoes and leather moccasins were possible alternatives—and a long belted jacket, called a *capot*. In the summer, handkerchiefs were some-times worn, turban-like, around the head, a fashion that became popular among the Creek Indians, as well. Women dressed in chemises, over which were worn cotton dresses or bodices and ankle-length skirts. They also wore aprons and shoes. Clothing for children followed the same pat-terns as adult dress.[91]

The fort garrison was supposed to be issued standard uniforms, for which an allowance was deducted from the soldiers' pay. Supplies from France, however, were frequently delayed and they must have had to substitute nonregulation items for elements of their uniforms on many oc-casions. For example, in 1710 Governor Bienville was reduced to distrib-uting deerskins to the soldiers in Mobile so that they could make shirts for themselves.[92] At the Alabama post in 1721, the soldiers received new uni-forms, but muskets did not arrive and some were armed with guns intended for the Indian trade instead.[93] In 1729, the supply problem remained a concern of the Fort Toulouse garrison. "Most of the time they lack their necessities, their pay, and their clothing. . . ."[94] And in 1745, the shortage of woolen shirts, trousers, stockings, and scarves was said to be affecting the morale of the garrison.[95]

Soldiers of *Les Compagnies Franches de la Marine* (troops recruited for garrison duty in French overseas colonies, distinct from marines who served on board ships) stationed in Louisiana were ordinarily issued two shirts with two collars, one pair of breeches, two pairs of woolen stockings, two pairs of shoes with double soles "of stout leather," one hat, one cravat, and two boxwood combs every year, with one greatcoat or one waistcoat distributed in alternate years.[96] The color and style of the uniforms were precisely specified in numerous regulations. In 1717, soldiers wore gray-white greatcoats lined and cuffed in blue, red waistcoats (later blue), blue breeches, black cravats, blue stockings, white canvas gaiters, and shoes. Sergeants had silver lace around the cuffs, and pewter buttons in contrast to the common soldier's brass buttons. Drummers customarily wore the "King's small livery": white chain lace on the crimson background of their coat linings and cuffs. All troops received cocked tricorn hats of black felt decorated along the brim with lace matching their button color, and displaying the black silk cockade of the colonial service.[97]

Officers' uniforms differed according to individual preference until 1733, when they too were standardized. In addition to the basic uniform worn by sergeants, an officer wore a sword and sash at the waist, a polished metal gorget—a vestige of medieval armor that adorned the throat—and a pure white greatcoat. Some high-ranking officers had scarlet coats, waistcoats, and breeches for full-dress occasions.[98]

Regular routine at most posts was for soldiers to answer reveille at 4 A.M., 6 A.M. in the winter, with evening retreat at 8 P.M. in the summer and 9 P.M. in the winter.[99] In an effort to prevent desertions, wax or tallow candles were used in the guardhouse and while making the rounds and calling roll in the evening. Elsewhere, candles were too expensive for everyday use, except by the mission priest.[100]

In addition to receiving a uniform, each soldier was also issued a number of accoutrements and weapons, including a hatchet, socket bayonet and scabbard with belt, powder horn and string, a cartridge box or shoulder pouch, and a flintlock musket.[101] Although a few pieces of the large .68 caliber (French 16 *calibre*) Tulle military muskets have been found at the Fort Toulouse site, most of the excavated gunparts are from lightweight muskets intended for the Indian trade.[102] These guns had smaller bores and contained mainly brass furnishings, rather than the iron triggerguards, sideplates, and buttplates found on military muskets.[103] Trade guns were widely used at French military outposts throughout Louisiana and Canada. The smaller caliber muskets conserved ammunition, and soldiers could be supplied from trade warehouses when military stores ran low.[104] English traders were another source of firearms, as is indicated by the fragments of English guns and the English-made gunflints found at the fort.[105]

•

An uncertain supply line from Mobile also contributed to shortages of foodstuffs at the Alabama post. Since the French could not grow wheat successfully in the region, flour had to be sent to Mobile from France, or later from French farms in Illinois, and then carried up river by bateaux to Fort Toulouse. To supplement this supply, the soldiers and settlers traded with the Indians for corn, beans, deer meat, bear oil (which substituted in Louisiana for olive oil), poultry and other native foods, a practice that proved mutually satisfactory and which was continued throughout the fort's occupation.[106] As explained by Governor Vaudreuil in 1745,

> we send nothing but flour for the subsistence of the garrison
> and which most frequently is in the situation of lacking it so
> that this garrison must necessarily trade in order to get a liv-
> ing, and it is likewise important that it be in that situation in
> order that the Indians may find a market for their products.[107]

Thus, colonial policy developed by making a virtue of necessity. Flour that otherwise would have gone to the Alabama post was sold in Mobile and the profits credited to the soldiers, who then were paid in merchandise, which enabled them to trade for provisions.[108]

The post inhabitants also quickly learned to raise their own crops and livestock. In 1721, they were experimenting with upland rice, corn, and tobacco.[109] The latter seems not to have been a success, but rice and corn soon became dietary mainstays.[110] Probably a garden, like the one that existed just outside the walls of Fort Tombecbé in 1763, furnished the post with vegetables such as cabbages, peas, beans, turnips, cucumbers, and onions, all carefully fertilized with nightsoil. And, no doubt a few apple trees were planted near the fort.[111]

By the 1740s, the French habitants at Fort Toulouse had cattle and hogs; both were damaging Indian crops, so Governor Vaudreuil urged the habitants to keep their livestock enclosed with fences and to consider a household limit of "three cattle and a pair of oxen for transport."[112] There is no evidence that such a limit was ever imposed, but the recommendation does suggest that cattle and hogs were permitted to roam free in the woods, where they could feed on mast and cane all winter.[113] The reference to oxen for transport implies that these animals were used during spring plowing and for drawing two-wheeled carts.[114] The cattle were a black Brittany strain brought from Canada; cows ranged from 700 to 900 pounds in size, and bulls could weigh up to 1,400 pounds.[115]

Although seldom mentioned in the documents, small "Creole hens" were kept at the fort from the first.[116] Horses could occasionally be purchased from English packhorse traders or from Indians, or were ridden overland from Mobile by officers.[117] There are no records of other domestic animals at the post, though one might surmise that certainly dogs, possibly sheep, and perhaps even pigeons were kept there.[118]

The amount of meat that different species contributed to the diet of Alabama post inhabitants can be determined from the animal bones found during archaeological excavations.[119] Bones from Fort Toulouse II, probably the food refuse of officers and officials who actually lived in the fort barracks, indicate that cattle contributed two-thirds of the meat, with the remaining amount coming mainly from white-tailed deer, still less from hogs, and miniscule quantities from fish and fowl. These proportions are remarkably similar to a bone sample collected in excavations in French Mobile, at a site also probably occupied by military officers. In comparison to these bone samples from high-status residences, the animal refuse from an Alabama post household, located several hundred yards to the east of the fort, provides an interesting contrast. At this presumably middle-class household, beef, venison, and pork each comprised about one-third of the available meat, supplemented by small amounts of fish (gar, catfish, and drum) and fowl (wild turkey and domestic chicken). Evidently, the habitants' and common soldiers' families that lived in the post village relied more on wild game and domestic hogs than on the more expensive cattle for their meat. The evidence from these sites indicates that French colonists in Louisiana ate more meat than their compatriots in France. By 1750, pork had virtually disappeared from the tables of the French peasantry because of high salt prices and shifts in agriculture toward more grain production; beef had always been beyond their means.[120]

Brandy was provided for troop rations and to compete effectively with English rum offered to the Indians in trade; the habitants generally did without and drank water.[121] Most brandy was shipped in wooden-hooped casks (containing 60 gallons) and kegs (15 gallons).[122] This sort of container leaves no physical trace for archaeologists to recover, so the only evidence for liquor at the post is some glass bottle fragments. These bottles once may have contained wine, which was required for mass by the mission priest, but the bottles must have been reused countless times for many other purposes long after the original contents had been consumed.[123]

•

Daniel Thomas's excellent discussion of trade still stands as one of the best available for French Louisiana.[124] As he mentions, French officials tried to hold the Indians to their interest by offering desirable goods at as low prices as possible. Some habitants at the Alabama post even seem to have made a cottage industry of earbob and spangle production by manufacturing these ornaments for the Indian trade from worn brass kettles.[125] Another tactic was to provide free gun repair by the fort gunsmith, a practice ruefully described by the English trader, Edmond Atkin.[126]

> When an Indian after undergoing the mortification of having a Gun (perhaps from trial and use become a favourite one) suddenly by some slight accident to the Lock, or Touch hole, render'd intirely useless to him, I say when he sees it afterwards as suddenly restored to its former State, and as usefull, as before, it gladdens his Heart more than a present of a new Gun would. He then looks on our Trader and the Frenchman with different Eyes. The former only Sold him the Gun (perhaps at an extravagant price); the latter when it is spoiled, hath as it were new made [it] for nothing. This endears the Frenchman to him. He is glad to have such a Friend near him. The mutual Convenience unites them.

However, shortages of trade goods at the Alabama post led not only the Indians, but also the French, to resort to English traders. In exchange for gunpowder, lead balls, brandy, and poor quality deerskins, the French received a greater variety of trade goods than they could have obtained from Mobile, and this commerce continued even during times of war between Britain and France.[127] Alabama Indians who had visited English trading houses were frequently persuaded to part with their newly acquired possessions for brandy.[128] The French then traded these goods back to the Indians for deerskins and provisions, or doled them out as presents to influential headmen.[129] By means of this illicit trade, the French also acquired scarce commodities for their own use, such as additional muskets and ceramic smoking pipes.[130]

•

Late in 1763, the French garrison and villagers began the long overland trek to Mobile after discarding many of their possessions and giving others to their old neighbors, the Alabama Indians.[131] The Alabamas moved their village of Taskigi to the abandoned fort site, where years later visitors saw broken cannons in front of the headman's house.[132]

Meanwhile, many of the Alabama emigrants had sailed to New Orleans in January, 1764, moved on to Pointe Coupée in March, and finally settled in Opelousas, on the right bank of Bayou Courtableau near present-day Washington, by the end of the year.[133] Several villages of Alabama Indians also decided to move away from English domination and settled along the Mississippi and Red rivers in Louisiana.[134]

When Colonel Marinus Willett "took a walk" in May, 1790, "to see the old French Alabama fort; or rather the place where it stood," he found "scarcely a trace of it to be seen at present."[135] Despite the persistent legend, recorded by historian Albert Pickett, that the old trenches at Fort Toulouse were cleaned out and reused by the American army engaged in constructing Fort Jackson in 1814, this was clearly not the case.[136] Archaeological research has established that Fort Jackson was built over the much smaller Fort Toulouse II (which had no moat), but did not incorporate any features of the earlier structure. In fact, a thick layer of clay was placed over the old fort site to level the ground surface. A garrison was maintained at Fort Jackson until 1818. William Bibb, governor of Alabama Territory, resided nearby and encouraged attempts in 1819 and 1820 to establish a town, to be named Jackson City, at the fort to serve as the state capital. The site of present-day Montgomery ultimately proved a more popular town location, however, and the old fort site was turned over to farming.[137]

•

In any objective analysis, one must conclude that the French establishment among the Alabamas was quite successful. From the French perspective, Fort Toulouse effectively limited English expansion toward Louisiana while continuously maintaining a modicum of French political and economic influence among the local Indian groups. The Indians, on the other hand, retained an alternative supply source for trade goods and another market for deerskins that allowed them to postpone for several decades their ultimate dependence on English trade.

Indian support of the French settlement went beyond mere tolerance of the colonial presence; they actively participated in numerous post-related ventures. Alabamas provided much of the labor and many of the materials used to construct both forts. The small tribes living in the vicinity of Mobile—the Apalachees, Naniabes, Tohomes, and Mobilians—frequently manned the oars on supply boats sent to Fort Toulouse, since soldiers detailed for that task frequently deserted to the English.[138]

So great an importance did the French place on maintaining peaceful relations with their Indian neighbors, that they instituted a policy of sending French boys to live in Indian villages to learn native languages and customs.[139] These individuals later served as interpreters, and their knowledge of Indian societies frequently aided post commandants.[140]

The advantages to be derived from individuals intimately acquainted with Indian customs can be seen in the strange case of Louis de Lantagnac. As a thirteen-year-old ensign stationed at Fort Toulouse, Lantagnac wandered away from the fort one day in the fall of 1745 (whether he intended to desert or just became lost in the woods is uncertain), and was captured by a band of Chickasaws. He spent the next three years in Charleston, where he gained the confidence and support of Governor Glen, who outfitted him for the Cherokee trade. Lantagnac traded with the Cherokees for the next six years, and had a son by an Indian woman with whom he lived at Great Tellico Town. While visiting a lower Creek town in December, 1754, he was approached by some Frenchmen and persuaded to return with them to Fort Toulouse in hopes of obtaining a pardon. Partly due to his knowledge of the Cherokees and partly because he was a kinsman of ex-Governor Vaudreuil, Lantagnac's long absence was forgiven and his rank restored. When the Cherokees prevented his Indian family from joining him, he began an energetic campaign to turn the Overhill Cherokees against the English. Lantagnac brought Mankiller of Tellico and other Cherokee leaders to Fort Toulouse on October 18, 1756, eventually going on to New Orleans, where they signed a treaty. So successful was Lantagnac in his negotiations with the Cherokees that the English offered a bounty for his scalp. But his supporters protected him and he continued to promote a pro-French faction among the Overhill Cherokees until the abandonment of Fort Toulouse.[141]

Perhaps one of the most unusual features of the Alabama post was the presence of a sizable French agricultural community nestled among a large Indian population. Elsewhere in Louisiana, major French settlements had few Indian neighbors nearby and these generally were weak tribes already severely reduced in numbers through disease and warfare. The one exception, a major colonizing effort among the Natchez from 1716 to 1729, had ended disastrously with a massacre of French settlers, precipitated by repeated demands for Indian-owned lands. Perhaps French colonial officials learned something from this hard lesson; afterward they seemed to have tried to avoid giving the Indians the impression that they coveted their lands. In this, the French differed from the English, as an interpreter at Fort Toulouse emphasized to the Creeks:

> . . . when is the Day that ever us, the French, encroached upon your Land? 'Tis true you lent us a Span of Land to build a Fort upon, and it is equally true, that we never offered, in the least, to encroach further than what you granted us.[142]

Fort Toulouse was principally a military post and trading enclave, but it probably could not have served these functions effectively, located in the midst of the Creek country, without the ties that developed between the Indians and the French civilians. As explained by Edmond Atkin:

> . . . it is commonly supposed, that the French have acquired their influence, and maintain their Power among the Indian Nations, intirely by their Forts; . . . yet it is truly a great absurdity to imagine, that either the French or ourselves can maintain an Interest & Influence, more especially among the Inland Indians, barely by the Possession of Forts, without being at the same time possess'd of their *Affections*. . . .[143]

•

Acknowledgments

I appreciate the assistance of Malcolm MacDonald and Judith Knight at The University of Alabama Press. My gratitude is also due Richard Krause and Ned Jenkins, who generously provided information on their recent excavations at Fort Toulouse. Additional information on contemporaneous Alabama and Creek Indian sites has been derived from research supported by the National Science Foundation under grants BNS-8305437, "Culture Change on the Creek Indian Frontier," and BNS-8507469, "Cataloging and Documenting the Historic Creek Archaeological Collections of the Alabama Department of Archives and History." The Alabama Historical Commission sponsored my excavations in 1980 and 1984, which were co-directed by Craig Sheldon. I thank all those students, park employees, and commission staff members who contributed to that work. Finally, I am most grateful to three individuals whose research has aided my own: Brian Wood, Robert Pratt, and, especially, Daniel Thomas.

•

Notes to Introduction

1. Dunbar Rowland and Albert G. Sanders, eds., *Mississippi Provincial Archives, French Dominion* (hereafter, *MPAFD*), Vol. I: *1729–1740* (Mississippi Department of Archives and History, Jackson, 1927), p. 253; Samuel C. Williams, ed., *Adair's History of the American Indians* (Watauga Press, Johnson City, Tennessee, 1930), p. 166; Thomas S. Woodward, *Woodward's Reminiscences of the Creeks, or Muscogee Indians* (Barnett & Wimbish, Montgomery, Alabama, 1859), p. 39.

2. Peter J. Hamilton, *Colonial Mobile* (Houghton Mifflin, Boston, 1897, revised edition, 1910); Charles E. A. Gayarré, *History of Louisiana, The French Domination*, Vols. I–IV (F. F. Hansell & Bros., New Orleans, 1903).

3. See, for example, *The Guarantee of Belgian Independence and Neutrality in European Diplomacy, 1830's–1930's* (D. H. Thomas Publishing, Kingston, Rhode Island, 1983); and *The New Guide to the Diplomatic Archives of Western Europe*, edited by D. H. Thomas and Lynn M. Case (University of Pennsylvania Press, Philadelphia, 1975); Thomas's last work in the realm of French colonial history resulted in the article, "Pre-Whitney Cotton Gins in French Louisiana," *The Journal of Southern History*, Vol. XXXI (1965), pp. 135–48.

4. There is no comprehensive monograph on excavations at Fort Toulouse. Several interim reports have been written and were issued in limited quantities: Donald P. Heldman, "Archaeological Investigations of Fort Toulouse: 1972–1973" (Alabama Historical Commission, Montgomery, 1973); Heldman, "Archaeological Investigations of Fort Toulouse: 1973–74 (Phase II)" (Alabama Historical Commission, Montgomery, 1976); B. McDonald Brooms and James W. Parker, "Fort Toulouse Phase III Completion Report" (Alabama Historical Commission, Montgomery, 1980); Brooms and Parker, "Fort Toulouse Phase IV Progress Report" (Alabama Historical Commission, Montgomery, 1980); Gregory A. Waselkov, Brian M. Wood, and Joseph M. Herbert, *Colonization and Conquest: The 1980 Archaeological Excavations at Fort Toulouse and Fort Jackson, Alabama* (Auburn University at Montgomery, 1982); Waselkov, *Fort Toulouse Studies* (Auburn University at Montgomery, 1984).

5. See the Barnwell Map of 1722, London, Public Record Office, Colonial Office Library, Maps, North American Colonies, Georgia 2; Wilbur R. Jacobs, ed., *The Appalachian Indian Frontier: The Edmond Atkin Report and Plan of 1755* (University of Nebraska Press, Lincoln, 1967), p. 59; Anonymous, *State of the British and French Colonies in North America* (A. Millar, London, 1755), p. 9; Theodore C. Pease, ed., "Anglo-French Boundary Disputes in the West, 1749–1763," *Illinois State Historical Library Collections*, Vol. XXVII (1936), p. 370.

6. Jay Higginbotham, *Old Mobile: Fort Louis de la Louisiane, 1702–1711* (Museum of the City of Mobile, 1977); William L. McDowell, Jr., ed., *Documents Relating to Indian Affairs, 1750–1754* (South Carolina Archives Department, Columbia, 1758), p. 49.

7. David H. Corkran, *The Creek Frontier, 1540–1783* (University of Oklahoma Press, Norman, 1967).

8. Rowland & Sanders, *MPAFD*, Vol. III (1932), p. 732; Allan D. Candler, ed., *The Colonial Records of the State of Georgia* (hereafter *CRSG*), Vol. XXIII (1914), pp. 432–33.

9. Richebourg G. McWilliams, ed., *Fleur de Lys and Calumet: Being the Pénicaut Narrative of French Adventure in Louisiana* (Louisiana State University Press, Baton Rouge, 1953), pp. 164–65; Seymour Feiler, ed., *Jean-Bernard Bossu's Travels in the Interior of North America, 1751–1762* (University of Oklahoma Press, Norman, 1962), pp. 143–44; Ben C. McCary, ed., *Memoirs of Louis Le-Clerc Milfort* (Beehive Press, Savannah, 1959), p. 117.

10. Florence G. Watts, ed., "The Rayneval Memorandum of 1782," *Indiana Magazine of History*, Vol. 38 (1942), pp. 167–207; Cecil Headlam, ed., *Calendar*

of State Papers, Colonial Series, America and West Indies, Vol. XXXI (London, 1933), p. 301.

11. Daniel H. Thomas, this volume, pp. 75–76; Archives of the Diocese of Mobile, Residence of the Archbishop of Mobile, Baptisms: Register A (1704–1778), Marriages: Register B (1726–1812), Burials: Register C (1726–1830); Milo B. Howard, Jr., and Robert R. Rea, eds., The Mémoire Justificatif of the Chevalier Montault de Monberaut (University of Alabama Press, Tuscaloosa, 1965), pp. 16–18, 70; Bill Barron, The Vaudreuil Papers (Polyanthos, New Orleans, 1975); Jacqueline Vidrine, ed., Love's Legacy: The Mobile Marriages, Recorded in French, Transcribed with Annotated Abstracts in English, 1724–1786 (University of Southwestern Louisiana, Lafayette, 1985).

The names of the Fort Toulouse commandants and their terms of service, as best as can be determined, are as follows:

Lieutenant Vitral [or Vitrac] de La Tour	1717–1720
Captain François Marchand de Coursalle [or Course1]	1720–1723
(served again)	1727–1730
Major Crépin de Pechon	1723–1727
Lieutenant Monmarquet	1731–1733
Lieutenant Jean Baptiste Benoît de St. Clair	1733–1734
Lieutenant Pierre Annibal Develle	1734–1735
Lieutenant Pierre Henri d'Ernville	1736–1738
(served again, as Captain)	1741–1742
(served again)	1746
Lieutenant François Marie Joseph Hazeur	1738–1741
(served again)	1745
Lieutenant Jean Richard Poilvilain de La Houssaye	1743–1745
Captain Jean Paul Le Sueur	1746–1749
Captain Louis de Bonnille	1749–1753
Lieutenant Louis Massée	1753–1755
Captain Montault de Monberaut	1755–1759
Captain Jean Baptiste Benoist Aubert	1759
Captain Jean Baptiste de Grandmaison	1760
Lieutenant de Lanouë Bogard	1760–1763

12. Council of Marine to l'Epinay, October 18, 1716, Paris, Archives Nationales, Archives des Colonies (hereafter, AC), Series B, Vol. 38, p. 340; Hamilton, Colonial Mobile (1910), p. 190.

13. Mark F. Boyd, "Documents Describing the Second and Third Expeditions of Lieutenant Diego Peña to Apalachee and Apalachicolo in 1717 and 1718," Florida Historical Quarterly Vol. 31 (1952), pp. 137–38.

14. Personal communications with Richard Krause and Ned Jenkins, 1988.

15. cf. McWilliams, Fleur de Lys, p. 165; the fort was "about 50 toises square. . . ."; a toise equals 6 feet 4¾ inches.

16. Robert G. McPherson, ed., The Journal of the Earl of Egmont, 1732–1738 (University of Georgia Press, Athens, 1962), p. 175; Rowland and Sanders, MPAFD, Vol. III (1932), p. 665.

17. Pauger to the Directors, March 23, 1725, Paris AC, C13A, Vol. 9, 371v; J. H. Easterby, ed., *The Journal of the Commons House of Assembly* (hereafter, *JCHA*), Vol. 7, *1746–1747* (South Carolina Archives Department, Columbia, 1958), p. 223; Jacobs, *Atkin Report*, p. 60.

18. Verner W. Crane, *The Southern Frontier, 1670–1732* (W. W. Norton & Co., New York, 1981), p. 191.

19. Brian M. Wood, "Fort Okfuskee: A British Challenge to Fort Toulouse aux Alibamons," in Waselkov, *Fort Toulouse Studies*, pp. 41–51; Easterby, *JCHA*, Vol. I, *1736–1739* (1951), pp. 78–79, 122; William L. Anderson and James A. Lewis, *A Guide to Cherokee Documents in Foreign Archives* (Scarecrow Press, Metuchen, New Jersey, 1983), p. 457.

20. Candler, *CRSG*, Vol. IV (1906), p. 325, Vol. XXI (1910), p. 289; Easterby, *JCHA*, Vol. I (1951), p. 95; Kenneth Coleman and Milton Ready, eds., *The Colonial Records of Georgia*, Vol. 20, *1732–1735* (University of Georgia Press, Athens, 1982), p. 310; Thomas overstated the case when he claimed that "no fort was built there at this or any other time," p. 17.

21. Candler, *CRSG*, Vol. IV (1906), p. 552; Larry E. Ivers, *British Drums on the Southern Frontier* (University of North Carolina Press, Chapel Hill, 1974), pp. 141, 188.

22. Jacobs, *Atkin Report*, p. 64; Easterby, *JCHA*, Vol. II (1952), p. 307, Vol. IV (1954), pp. 447, 492; Williams, *Adair's History*, p. 279.

23. Easterby, *JCHA*, Vol. V (1955), p. 222.

24. Dunbar Rowland, A. G. Sanders, and Patricia K. Galloway, eds., *MPAFD*, Vol. IV, *1729–1748* (Louisiana State University Press, Baton Rouge, 1984), pp. 246, 256.

25. Wood, "Fort Okfuskee," pp. 48–49.

26. Most of the following discussion is derived from Waselkov, *Fort Toulouse Studies*, pp. 3–16.

27. Brooms and Parker, "Phase IV," p. 14.

28. Elisabeth S. Sheldon, "Plant Remains from the Southeastern Bastion of Fort Jackson" (Report to the Alabama Historical Commission, Montgomery, 1980).

29. Rowland and Sanders, *MPAFD*, Vol. III (1932), p. 665.

30. *Ibid.*; Samuel Wilson, Jr., "Colonial Fortifications and Military Architecture in the Mississippi Valley," in J. F. McDermott, ed., *The French in the Mississippi Valley* (University of Illinois Press, Urbana, 1965), fig. 19.

31. William L. McDowell, Jr., ed., *Documents Relating to South Carolina Indian Affairs, 1754–1765* (University of South Carolina Press, Columbia, 1970), p. 299.

32. Samuel Wilson, Jr., "Architecture in Eighteenth-Century West Florida," in Samuel Proctor, ed., *Eighteenth-Century West Florida and Its Borderlands* (University Presses of Florida, Gainesville, 1975), p. 106.

33. William A. Hunter, *Forts on the Pennsylvania Frontier, 1753–1758* (Pennsylvania Historical and Museum Commission, Harrisburg, 1960), p. 111; James W. Parker, "Archaeological Test Investigations at 1Su7: The Fort Tombecbé Site," *Journal of Alabama Archaeology*, Vol. 28 (1982), fig. 3; Rowland, Sanders, and Galloway, *MPAFD*, Vol. V (1984), p. 254.

34. John B. Fortier, "New Light on Fort Massac," in J. F. McDermott, ed., *Frenchmen and French Ways in the Mississippi Valley* (University of Illinois Press, Urbana, 1969), p. 62.

35. Brooms and Parker, "Phase IV," pp. 17–19; Waselkov, *Fort Toulouse Studies*, pp. 12–16.

36. Personal communications with Richard Krause and Ned Jenkins, 1988.

37. Samuel Wilson, Jr., "Gulf Coast Architecture," in E. F. Dibble and E. W. Newton, eds., "Spain and Her Rivals on the Gulf Coast," *Gulf Coast History and Humanities Conference Proceedings*, Vol. 2 (1971), fig. 10; Samuel Wilson, Jr., "Religious Architecture in French Colonial Louisiana," *Winterthur Portfolio*, Vol. 8 (1973), pp. 64, 68; Wilson, "West Florida," p. 106.

38. Wilson, "Colonial Fortification," fig. 10; Thomas, this volume, p. 11; Donald P. Heldman and William L. Minnerly, "The Powder Magazine at Fort Michilimackinac: Excavation Report," *Reports in Mackinac History and Archaeology*, Vol. 6 (1977), pp. 6, 23; Walter J. Saucier and Katherine W. Seineke, "François Saucier, Engineer of Fort de Chartres, Illinois," in McDermott, *French Ways*, fig. 3.

39. Thomas, this volume, p. 11.

40. Although the buttresses supporting the Fort Toulouse magazine probably indicate a vaulted ceiling, with its exceptional load-bearing capacity, the Fort Condé barracks in Mobile are known to have had props and buttresses "to maintain the building against wind storms and at the same time . . . to make [the walls] plumb." Heloise H. Cruzat, "Records of the Superior Council of Louisiana," *Louisiana Historical Quarterly* (hereafter, "RSCL" *LSQ*), Vol. 8 (1925), pp. 298–99.

41. Alan Kemper and Michael Emrick, *Planning Documents for the Restoration of the Old Spanish Fort, Pascagoula, Mississippi* (Building Conservation Technology, Inc., Nashville, Tennessee, 1980).

42. Margaret K. Brown and Lawrie C. Dean, *The Village of Chartres in Colonial Illinois, 1720–1765* (Polyanthos, New Orleans, 1977), p. 653.

43. *Ibid.*, p. 719.

44. Charles E. Peterson, "The Houses of French St. Louis," in J. F. McDermott, ed., *The French in the Mississippi Valley* (University of Illinois Press, Urbana, 1965), pp. 26–27; bricks were often used in *colombage* construction, too.

45. John A. Walthall and Elizabeth D. Benchley, "The River L'Abbé Mission," *Illinois Historic Preservation Agency, Studies in Illinois Archaeology*, Vol. 2 (1987), p. 27; Wilson, "Religious Architecture," fig. 34.

46. The results of the elemental analysis by X-ray emission spectrography demonstrate that the French bricks and local clay are very similar in their percentages of seven chemical constituents, in most cases so similar as to be statistically indistinguishable. As a further test, iron-manganese inclusions present in both the local clay and the bricks were also analyzed and, again, their elemental makeups are very much alike.

Element	Brick 1	Brick 2	Brick 3	Clay	Inclusions Clay	Inclusions Brick
Al_2O_3	15.05	17.70	18.20	19.00	19.80	19.34
SiO_2	72.40	70.00	71.50	68.53	64.74	56.26
K_2O	2.02	1.82	1.77	1.91	2.04	2.30
Fe_2O_3	6.94	7.27	6.87	7.45	10.44	17.11
CaO	0.19	0.22	0.36	0.24	0.24	0.28
TiO_2	1.06	1.00	1.05	1.05	1.02	0.91
ZrO*	–	+	+	+	+	–
Mn*					+	+

*Presence/absence only

47. David A. Harris and Jerry J. Nielsen, "Archaeological Salvage Excavations at the Site of the French Fort Condé, Mobile, Alabama" (University of Alabama, Tuscaloosa, 1972), p. 32; Craig T. Sheldon, Jr., and John W. Cottier, *Origins of Mobile* (Auburn University at Montgomery, 1983), p. 77; the average dimensions of Fort Toulouse II bricks are 8⅜ inches long, 4⅛ inches wide, and 2¹⁄₁₆ inches thick.

48. Joseph A. Foster, ed., "Accounts of Brickmaking in England Published in the 17th and 18th Centuries," *Contribution to a Study of Brickmaking in America, Part 3* (Claremont, 1965).

49. Lise Boily and Jean-François Blanchette, *The Bread Ovens of Quebec* (National Museums of Canada, Ottawa, 1979); Fred Kniffen, "The Outdoor Oven in Louisiana," *Louisiana History*, Vol. 1 (1960), p. 28.

50. Brown and Dean, *Village of Chartres*, pp. 345, 365.

51. Pierre Goubert, *The French Peasantry in the Seventeenth Century* (Cambridge University Press, Cambridge, 1986), p. 41.

52. Headlam, *Calendar*, Vol. XXXI (1932), p. 362.

53. Rowland and Sanders, *MPAFD*, Vol. III (1932), p. 564; K. G. Davies, ed., *Calendar of State Papers, Colonial Series, America and West Indies*, Vol. XLI (1953), p. 170.

54. Albert Manucy, "Artillery Through the Ages," *U.S. Department of the Interior, National Park Service, Interpretive Series, History*, Vol. 3 (1949), frontispiece, p. 37; one of these breechblocks, a 10-inch-long specimen made of brass, was found at the fort site in the late nineteenth century and is now owned by a private collector in Wetumpka. The bore of this piece is about 2 inches in diameter, the caliber of a French one-pound shot; John Muller, *A Treatise of Artillery*, facsimile reprint of 1780 edition (Museum Restoration Service, Bloomfield, Ontario, 1977), p. 10; illustrated in Hamilton, *Colonial Mobile* (1910), facing p. 192.

55. Jacobs, *Atkin Report*, p. 60.

56. Barron, *Vaudreuil Papers*, p. 414; Vaudreuil to Le Sueur, January 24, 1747, Huntington Library, LO 9, Vol. III, p. 250.

57. McDowell, *Indian Affairs, 1754–1765*, p. 299; cf. William L. Saunders, ed., *The Colonial Records of North Carolina*, Vol. V (Raleigh, 1887), p. 467.

58. e.g. Feiler, *Bossu's Travels*, pp. 151–52; McDowell, *Indian Affairs, 1754–1765*, p. 68.

59. Mark Van Doren, ed., *Travels of William Bartram* (Macy-Masius, New York, 1928), p. 355.

60. C. L. Grant, ed., *Letters, Journals, and Writings of Benjamin Hawkins*, Vol. I (Beehive Press, Savannah, 1980), p. 297, cf. p. 25.

61. Albert J. Pickett, *History of Alabama* (Walker and James, Charleston, 1851), p. 195; Hamilton, *Colonial Mobile* (1910), p. 192.

62. Muller, *Treatise*, p. 10.

63. Heldman, "Fort Toulouse, 1972–1973," pp. 154–55, fig. 69D; Brooms and Parker, "Phase IV," p. 12.

64. Louis de Toussard, *American Artillerist's Companion or Elements of Artillery*, Vol. I, reprint of 1809 edition (Greenwood Press, New York, 1969), p. 147; Muller, *Treatise*, p. 10.

65. Brooms and Parker, "Phase III," p. 141; personal communication with William P. Roberts II, 1987; also see Douglas Bryce, *Weaponry from the Machault, an 18th-Century French Frigate* (Parks Canada, Ottawa, 1984), pp. 47, 51.

66. Dunbar Rowland, ed., *Mississippi Provincial Archives, English Dominion, 1763–1766* (herafter, *MPAED*) (Brandon Publishing, Nashville, 1911), p. 38.

67. Muller, *Treatise*, pp. 94, 98; de Toussard, *Artillerist's Companion*, Vol. II, pp. 312, 316.

68. cf. Rowland, *MPAED*, p. 38.

69. Candler, *CRSG*, Vol. VII (1906), p. 134; Vol II (1904), p. 414.

70. Jean Delanglez, "The French Jesuits in Lower Louisiana (1700–1763)," *Catholic University, Studies in American Church History*, Vol. XXI (1935), p. 403; Charles R. Maduell, Jr., *The Census Tables for the French Colony of Louisiana from 1699 through 1732* (Genealogical Publishing Co., Baltimore, 1972), p. 27, 1721 census; Note that Thomas (p. 79, n. 10) was in error regarding the Census of Acadians at Post Toulouse, dating to 1758 (Paris, AC, C13A, Vol. 40, 157–157v). This document, which refers to an Acadian settlement in Nova Scotia, was misfiled with Louisiana papers by a clerk in France and has been a source of confusion for many researchers; e.g., Jacqueline K. Voorhies, ed., *Some Late Eighteenth Century Louisianans, Census Records: 1758–1796* (University of Southern Louisiana, Lafayette, 1973), pp. 421–22; Waselkov, Wood, and Herbert, *Colonization and Conquest*, pp. 76–80; Johnnie Andrews, Jr., *Fort Toulouse Colonials, 1717–1823* (Bienville Historical Society, Prichard, Alabama, 1987); and others.

71. Paris, AC, D2C, Vols. 51–52; Archives of the Diocese of Mobile, Registers A–C; Vidrine, *Love's Legacy, passim*.

72. Based mainly on Waselkov, Wood, and Herbert, *Colonization and Conquest*; Andrews, *Fort Toulouse Colonials*; Jacqueline O. Vidrine and Elaine G. Puchen, "The First Fontenot Families," *Louisiana Genealogical Register*, Vol. 22 (1975), pp. 387–91, Vol. 23 (1976), pp. 122–23.

73. Rowland, Sanders, and Galloway, *MPAFD*, Vol. IV (1984), p. 173; Vaudreuil to the Minister, April 28, 1751, Paris, AC, C13A, Vol. 35, pp. 78–79.

74. Andrew S. Walsh and Robert V. Wells, "Population Dynamics in the Eighteenth-Century Mississippi River Valley: Acadians in Louisiana," *Journal of Social History*, Vol. 11 (1978), p. 523.

75. Johnnie Andrews, Jr., ed., *Mobile Church Records, 1704–1813: A Partially Reconstructed List* (privately printed, 1967).

76. Marcel Giraud, *A History of French Louisiana*, Vol. I, *The Reign of Louis XIV, 1698–1715* (Louisiana State University Press, Baton Rouge, 1974), p. 233.

77. Charles E. O'Neill, *Church and State in French Colonial Louisiana* (Yale University Press, New Haven, 1966).

78. Pickett, *History of Alabama*, pp. 343–44; cf. Woodward, *Reminiscences*, p. 53; Hamilton, *Colonial Mobile* (1910), p. 191. La Houssaye and Le Sueur were accused of raping Indian women; Vaudreuil to La Houssaye, December 7, 1743, Huntington Library, LO9, Vol. III, p. 28; Patricia K. Galloway, "Louisiana Post Letters: The Missing Evidence for Indian Diplomacy," *Louisiana History*, Vol. 22 (1981), p. 35.

79. Archives of the Diocese of Mobile, Register A, Baptisms, July 22, 1750.

80. At least 17 soldiers were eventually linked by marriage alliances; also see Carl J. Ekberg, *Colonial Ste. Geneviève* (Patrice Press, Gerald, Missouri, 1986), p. 36.

81. Vaughan B. Baker, "Les Louisianaises: A Reconnaissance," in James J. Cooke, ed., *Proceedings of the Fifth Meeting of the French Colonial Historical Society* (University Press of America, Lanham, Maryland, 1980), p. 11.

82. Frequencies of marriages, births, and deaths, by month:

Month	Marriages	Births	Deaths
January	2	6	2
February	1	6	2
March	0	3	3
April	3	4	2
May	3	0	1
June	1	1	1
July	0	0	1
August	0	3	3
September	1	1	2
October	0	0	6
November	0	0	3
December	0	3	1
Totals	11	27	27

83. Goubert, *French Peasantry*, p. 66.

84. For two examples, see Vidrine, *Love's Legacy*, pp. 56–59.

85. One inventory of an Alabama post inhabitant, Laurent Laurent, has survived, but it lists possessions in his home in Mobile, where he resided for a year before his death in 1737. Cruzat, "RSCL," *LHQ*, Vol. 9 (1926) p. 503; Louisiana Historical Center, Records of the Superior Council of Louisiana, Inventory of Succession of Laurent Laurent, August 17, 1737 (8641)(2154), 10 pp.

86. Natalia M. Belting, *Kaskaskia Under the French Regime* (Polyanthos, New Orleans, 1975), pp. 43–46.

87. Ibid., p. 45; Henry P. Dart, "Gentleman of Pointe Coupée, 1743," *Louisiana Historical Quarterly*, Vol. 5 (1922), p. 469; Cruzat, "RSCL," *LHQ*, Vol. 12 (1929), p. 652.

88. Belting, *Kaskaskia*, p. 44; Dart, "A Gentleman," p. 469; Antoine Simon Le Page Du Pratz, *The History of Louisiana* (T. Becket, London, 1774), p. 342; Brooms and Parker, "Phase III," p. 109; Waselkov, *Fort Toulouse Studies*, pp. 27, 97.

89. Waselkov, Wood, and Herbert, *Colonization and Conquest*, pp. 143–47; Waselkov, *Fort Toulouse Studies*, p. 28.

90. Jean Chapelot, "La Céramique Exportée au Canada Français," *Dossiers de L'Archéologie (Dijon)*, Vol. 27 (1978), p. 107; M. L. Solon, *A History and Description of the Old French Faience* (Cassell and Co., London, 1903), p. 70; also see "RSCL," *LHQ*, Vol. 4 (1921), pp. 338–41.

91. Belting, *Kaskaskia*, p. 48; for a discussion of colonial French dress aimed at "Living History" afficionados, see Mary M. Johnson, Judy Forbes, and Kathy Delaney, *Historic Colonial French Dress* (Ouabache Press, West Lafayette, Indiana, 1982).

92. Rowland and Sanders, *MPAFD*, Vol. III (1932), p. 152.

93. Extract from Deliberations, June 28, 1721, Vincennes, AG, A1, 2592, no. 17.

94. Rowland, Sanders, and Galloway, *MPAFD*, Vol. IV (1984), p. 27.

95. Barron, *Vaudreuil Papers*, p. 367.

96. Rowland and Sanders, *MPAFD*, Vol. II (1929), p. 124; Rowland, Sanders, and Galloway, *MPAFD*, Vol. IV (1984), pp. 227–28.

97. René Chartrand, "The Troops of French Louisiana, 1699–1769," *Military Collector & Historian*, Vol. 25 (1973), p. 59; Bruce J. Egli, "French Marine Uniforms in North America." *F & I War*, Vol. 2 (1984), pp. 12–18.

98. Chartrand, "Troops," p. 61; Rowland and Sanders, *MPAFD*, Vol. III (1932), p. 621.

99. Blaine Adams, "The Construction and Occupation of the Barracks of the King's Bastion at Louisbourg," *Canadian Historic Sites: Occasional Papers in Archaeology and History*, Vol. 18 (1978), pp. 95–98.

100. Rowland and Sanders, *MPAFD*, Vol. III (1932), p. 395; Goubert, *French Peasantry*, p. 39.

101. Chartrand, "Troops," pp. 59–60.

102. T. M. Hamilton, *Colonial Frontier Guns* (The Fur Press, Chadron, Nebraska, 1980), pp. 29–62.

103. French musket balls from three excavations at Fort Toulouse are of the following sizes.

1 .512″ (French 38 *calibre*)
1 .544″ (32 *calibre*)
2 .550″ (30 *calibre*)

    2 .566″ (28 *calibre*)
    3 .580″ (26 *calibre*)

Waselkov, Wood, and Herbert, *Colonization and Conquest*, p. 181; Waselkov, *Fort Toulouse Studies*, pp. 35–37; Robert W. Pratt, "Analysis of a Late French Feature Located Near Fort Toulouse," in Waselkov, *Fort Toulouse Studies*, p. 75. Similar figures are reported from other French colonial sites; Hamilton, *Colonial Frontier Guns*, p. 135; Judy D. Tordoff, "An Archaeological Perspective on the Organization of the Fur Trade in Eighteenth-Century New France" (Ph.D. dissertation, Department of Anthropology, Michigan State University, 1983), pp. 78, 326.

    104. Barron, *Vaudreuil Papers*, p. 387.

    105. Waselkov, Wood, and Herbert, *Colonization and Conquest*, pp. 176–81; Waselkov, *Fort Toulouse Studies*, pp. 35–37; Pratt, "Late French Feature," pp. 75–77.

    106. Extract from Deliberations, June 1720, Memoir, Vincennes, AG, A1, 2592; Crane, *Southern Frontier*, p. 258; Heloise H. Crozat, ed., "Louisiana in 1724: Banet's Report," *Louisiana Historical Quarterly*, Vol. 12 (1929), p. 126; O'Neill, *Church and State*, pp. 202–203; Delanglez, "French Jesuits," p. 234; Candler, *CRSG*, Vol. VI (1906), pp. 341–42; Nancy M. Surrey, "The Commerce of Louisiana During the French Regime, 1699–1763," *Columbia University, Studies in the Social Sciences*, Vol. 167 (1916), p. 262.

    107. Rowland, Sanders, and Galloway, *MPAFD*, Vol. IV (1984), p. 250.

    108. Rowland and Sanders, *MPAFD*, Vol. III (1932), p. 590.

    109. Maduell, *Census Tables*, 1721 Census.

    110. Surrey, "Commerce," p. 170; Rowland, Sanders, and Galloway, *MPAFD*, Vol. IV (1984), p. 173.

    111. Rowland, *MPAED*, p. 25; Belting, *Kaskaskia*, p. 47; Goubert, *French Peasantry*, p. 13; Van Doren, *Travels*, p. 355.

    112. Vaudreuil to La Houssaye, November 2, 1743, Huntington Library, LO9, Vol. III, pp. 16–18; Barron, *Vaudreuil Papers*, p. 362.

    113. Thomas Campbell, "Thomas Campbell to Lord Deane Gordon: An Account of the Creek Indian Nation, 1764," *Florida Historical Quarterly*, Vol. 8 (1930), pp. 157, 160.

    114. Belting, *Kaskaskia*, p. 53.

    115. Campbell, "An Account," p. 160; Capt. Robert's Map of West Florida, 1772, Birmingham Public Library, Birmingham, Alabama; John E. Rouse, *World Cattle*, Vol. III, *Cattle of North America* (University of Oklahoma Press, Norman, 1973), pp. 266, 270–75, 504–505; Lyman Carrier, *The Beginnings of Agriculture in America* (McGraw-Hill, New York, 1923), p. 255.

    116. Diron d'Artaguette to Périer, September 3, 1729, Paris, AC, C13A, Vol. 12, p. 166.

    117. Vaudreuil to the Court, October 10, 1751, Huntington Library, LO9, Vol. II, p. 159.

    118. Rowland, *MPAED*, p. 24; Surrey, "Commerce," p. 284.

    119. Percentages of Available Meat from Excavated Samples of Animal Bones:

	Fort Toulouse	Alabama Post Household	French Mobile
Domestic Cattle	65.8	31.1	60.1
White-tailed Deer	20.7	32.7	24.0
Domestic Hog	10.3	31.1	11.3
Fowl	0.9	2.1	1.7
Fish	1.2	1.5	2.4
Total Bones	5,892	2,968	962
Minimum Number of Individuals	64	53	34

Sources: Waselkov, *Fort Toulouse Studies*, pp. 30–31, 96; Gregory A. Waselkov, "Analysis of Selected Samples of Bone from French Contexts, 1MB156," in Sheldon and Cottier, *Origins of Mobile*, p. 170.

120. Jean-Jacques Hemardinquer, "The Family Pig of the Ancien Régime: Myth or Fact," in R. Foster and O. Ranum, eds., *Food and Drink in History* (Johns Hopkins University Press, Baltimore, 1979), pp. 55–56.

121. "RSCL," *LHQ*, Vol. 5 (1922), p. 425.

122. Surrey, "Commerce," p. 162; Cruzat, "RSCL," *LHQ*, Vol. 17 (1934), pp. 569, 571; Tordoff, "Fur Trade," p. 72.

123. Rowland and Sanders *MPAFD*, Vol. II (1929), p. 483.

124. Also see Surrey, "Commerce," pp. 335–66; Paul C. Phillips, *The Fur Trade* (University of Oklahoma Press, Norman, 1961), Vol. I, pp. 361–76, 404–30, 448–83, 536–40; Daniel H. Usner, Jr., "The Deerskin Trade in French Louisiana," in Philip P. Boucher, ed., *Proceedings of the Tenth Meeting of the French Colonial Historical Society* (University Press of America, Lanham, Maryland, 1985).

125. Waselkov, *Fort Toulouse Studies*, p. 98.

126. McDowell, *Indian Affairs, 1754–1765*, p. 372; Jacobs, *Atkin Report*, pp. 9–10, 63–64.

127. Letters, September 3, 1729, Paris, AC, C13A, Vol. 12, pp. 161–71v; Ivers, *British Drums*, p. 189; Jacobs, *Atkin Report*, p. 23; Williams, *Adair's History*, p. 343; McDowell, *Indian Affairs, 1754–1765*, p. 366; Surrey, "Commerce," p. 449.

128. McDowell, *Indian Affairs, 1750–1754*, p. 312.

129. Jacobs, *Atkin Report*, p. 12.

130. All of the white clay pipes found at Fort Toulouse are of English manufacture, in contrast to high proportions of Dutch pipes found at Mobile, Port Dauphin, and Fort St. Pierre; Brooms and Parker, "Phase III," p. 137; Waselkov, Wood, and Herbert, *Colonization and Conquest*, pp. 175–76; Sheldon and Cottier, *Origins of Mobile*, pp. 130–31; Noel R. Stowe, "Archaeological Excavations at Port Dauphin," *University of South Alabama, Archaeological Research Series No. 1* (1977), pp. 105–109; Ian W. Brown, "Excavations at Fort St. Pierre," *Conference on Historic Site Archaeology Papers*, Vol. 9 (1975), pp. 69–72.

131. Corkran, *Creek Frontier*, p. 236; Campbell, "An Account," p. 160; the many black cattle owned by Alabamas in 1765 may have been, to a large extent, livestock abandoned by the French.

132. Van Doren, *Travels*, p. 355; McCary, *Milfort*, pp. 118, 128; Grant, *Benjamin Hawkins*, Vol. I, p. 25; Rowland, *MPAED*, p. 18; Corkran, *Creek Frontier*, p. 243; a midden accumulation in the vicinity of the western palisade dates to this period of occupation.

133. Carl A. Brasseaux, *A Comparative View of French Louisiana, 1699 and 1762* (University of Southwestern Louisiana, Lafayette, 1979), p. 108; Brasseaux, "Opelousas and the Alabama Immigrants, 1763–1766," *Attakapas Gazette*, Vol. XIV (1979); Brasseaux, *The Founding of New Acadia: The Beginnings of Acadian Life in Louisiana, 1765–1803* (Louisiana State University Press, Baton Rouge, 1987), p. 74; Captain Philip Pitman, *The Present State of the European Settlements on the Mississippi*, facsimile reprint of 1770 edition (Memphis State University Press, Memphis, 1977), p. 36; Walter Lowrie, ed., *American State Papers: Public Lands*, Vol. II, *1789–1834* (Duff Green, Washington, 1834), pp. 668–735, lists numerous members of the Fonteneau, Brignac, Doucet, and Lafleur families that held Spanish grants in Opelousas County. Some descendants of Fort Toulouse occupants still live in the vicinity of Kinder, Louisiana.

134. William A. Read, "Louisiana Place-Names of Indian Origin," *Louisiana State University Bulletin*, Vol. 19 (1927), pp. 4–5; Pitman, *European Settlements*, p. 24; Daniel Jacobson, "The Origin of the Koasati Community of Louisiana," *Ethnohistory*, Vol. 7 (1960), pp. 102–105; John R. Swanton, "Early History of the Creek Indians and Their Neighbors," *Smithsonian Institution, Bureau of American Ethnology, Bulletin*, Vol. 73 (1922), pp. 198–99.

135. William M. Willett, *A Narrative of the Military Action of Colonel Marinus Willett* (G. & C. & H. Carvill, New York, 1831), p. 104.

136. Pickett, *History of Alabama*, p. 593; Hamilton, *Colonial Mobile* (1910), p. 424; Thomas, this volume, p. 67; for the fate of the Creek towns in the vicinity of the Fort Toulouse site in the aftermath of the Creek War, see Gregory A. Waselkov and Brian M. Wood, "The Creek War of 1813–1814: Effects on Creek Society and Settlement Pattern," *Journal of Alabama Archaeology*, Vol. 32 (1986), pp. 1–24.

137. Waselkov, Wood, and Herbert, *Colonization and Conquest*, pp. 213–14.

138. Rowland, Sanders, and Galloway, *MPAFD*, Vol. V (1984), pp. 224–25; Feiler, *Bossu's Travels*, p. 128.

139. Rowland, Sanders, and Galloway, *MPAFD*, Vol. IV (1984), p. 100. This institution began in 1669 with a decree by Colbert to select French boys [*enfans de langue*, children of language] to be sent to the Levant where they would learn the native tongues; Charles W. Cole, *Colbert and a Century of French Mercantilism*, Vol. I (Columbia University Press, New York, 1939), p. 397.

140. Op. cit., pp. 100, 201–202 n4; Barron, *Vaudreuil Papers*, p. 368; Feiler, *Bossu's Travels*, p. 154.

141. John R. Alden, *John Stuart and the Southern Colonial Frontier* (Gordian Press, New York, 1944), pp. 52 n42, 61, 63, 128–29; McDowell, *Indian Affairs*,

1750–1754, pp. 40, 219, 225; Chevalier de Lantagnac to Governor Kerlerec, October 7, 1755, Paris, AC, C13A, Vol. 39, pp. 40–44v; Rowland, Sanders, and Galloway, *MPAFD*, Vol. V (1984), p. 166 n6.

142. McDowell, *Indian Affairs, 1750–1754*, p. 58; also see Alden, *John Stuart*, p. 15.

143. Jacobs, *Atkin Report*, pp. 8–9.

Fort Toulouse

NEW FRANCE

Quebec

Montreal

Ft. Michili-mackinac

NEW YORK

Boston

Ft. Detroit

Ft. Duquesne

ILLINOIS

Ft. Ouiatenon

Ft. de Chartres

VIRGINIA

Williamsburg

Ft. Massac

CHEROKEES

CAROLINA

Arkansas Post

CHICKASAWS

CREEKS

Ft. Okfuskee

Charleston

LOUISIANA

Ft. Tombecbe

CHOCTAWS

Ft. Toulouse

New Orleans

Mobile

St. Augustine

FLORIDA

Major French, English, and Spanish settlements in eastern North America.

FORT TOULOUSE

Fort Toulouse was constructed by the French in 1717 and was maintained as an alvanced post of the colony of Louisiana until 1763. It was located on the Coosa River near the junction of that stream and the Tallapoosa; thus it was at the head of the Alabama, four miles south of Wetumpka, Alabama and ten miles north of Montgomery. There have been many misconceptions about the fort, including even the date of construction and the very purposes for its establishment, not to mention traditions which are as romantic as they are false. The monument marking the site is the authority for the statement that it was "a defence against the Indians," whereas it would have been more accurate to say that it had national and even international significance in the rivalry of France and Great Britain for what is now the southeastern states. In fact, it may be said to have been a move in the game of power politics between the three greatest empires with the whole of North America at stake.

The Spanish held the Florida peninsula as the eighteenth century began and were seeking to extend their influence over the Indians to the north in what is now southern Georgia and southeast Alabama. Pensacola was His Most Catholic Majesty's leading post in western Florida.

The English colonies along the Atlantic seaboard had extended as far as the Carolinas with Charles Town, later to be called Charleston, as their southernmost port of significance. Successful efforts to establish the colony of Georgia would come in 1733.

French leaders, versed in geo-politics, dreamed of a long-range plan to encompass the English settlements, ringing them with forts in Canada, down the Ohio and Mississippi, and along the Gulf of Mexico. Louis XIV, the "Sun King" of France who outshone the other rulers until his death in 1715, paused long enough in his aggressive wars to send out Lemoyne, Sieur d'Iberville, who founded Fort Louis de la Mobile in 1702. This was only a short distance west of Spanish Pensacola; it was at the mouth of the Alabama-Tombigbee-Mobile river system where British traders were dominant upstream. Thus the rivals who had already fought vicious wars over other American territory, had made contact in the southeast. Anglo-French rivalry would be intensified and Fort Toulouse would have a significant role in this, the final phase of the contest.

A detail of Baron de Crenay's 1733 map of the Fort Toulouse area at the period of the occupancy of the French in the interior. ("Carte de partie de la Louisiane," Louisiane No. 1, courtesy of the Ministere de Colonies, Paris).

1. *The Potentialities of a Fort at the Head of the Alabama River*

> By establishing Fort Toulouse, the French "secured the most valuable strategic position in the whole southwestern country" of the colonial period. (Alfred W. Reynolds, "The Alabama-Tombigbee Basin in International Relations, 1701-1763.")

A French ring of forts around the English colonies would be an effort at "containment," or as one French contemporary expressed it, a "girdle" around these rivals. In one sense it was a giant pincer movement, and Fort Toulouse was the southeasternmost prong. The other prong was not so clear — at times it might appear to be Beausejour in the peninsula leading to Nova Scotia, or Crown Point on the southern shore of Lake Champlain, or, eventually, Fort Duquesne, which the British would call Fort Pitt, at the head of the Ohio River.

The site of the fort was ideal for the purpose, or as Verner Crane has written, "the most valuable strategic possession on the Carolina-Louisiana border . . ."[1] Alfred Wade Reynolds concluded independently that it was "the most valuable strategic position in the whole southwestern country"[2] of that era. It was some 170 miles northeast of Mobile, although much further via the rivers which slowly wound their way through the south Alabama plains. The particular site chosen was four miles above the head of the Alabama and the Coosa where this stream and the Tallapoosa approach within several hundred yards of each other, then diverged to form the lower portion of the peninsula.[3] The post was placed on the high bank of the latter stream which is the larger. It drains an immense area of northeast Alabama, northwestern Georgia, and eastern Tennessee. The Tallapoosa flows through the area to the east of the Coosa basin having its headwaters in eastern Tennessee also. They are separated by one of the southernmost ranges of the Appalachian highlands. Thus the fort was just below the hill country. It was athwart one of the two main routes taken by Charleston traders to this area. This was the Lower Path which skirted the hills; it then divided, with one branch leading almost due west to Choctaw country, and another northwest into the Chickasaw lands. The site was twenty-seven days distance from Charleston by packhorse, but only five days from Mobile, if going down by boat.

The site is such a natural location for settlement that it must have been used as long as man has lived in the area. Several Indian villages were grouped in the triangle of land between the rivers but further archaeological study will be necessary to determine just how many earlier cultures chose the same site. When the famed botanist, William Bartram visited it in 1777, he found the land to be "most fertile and delightful" along the rivers. He wrote that the "level plain between the conflux of the two majestic rivers" was "perhaps one of the most eligible situations for a city in the world; . . ."[4]

Later, the French officials would encourage settlement of civilians, but at this time they had more immediate interests. If the English fortified the site, they could make Mobile untenable and Mobile was itself an outpost protecting the mouth of the invaluable Mississippi. In French hands, a post could help protect the Gulf possessions and "contain" the English of Carolina, perhaps even set up a contrary movement which might push their rivals back into the sea.

There was also the extensive trade with the Indians of the whole area, a trade which had been monopolized by the business men of

Albion. The natives were developing an insatiable desire for European commodities for which they would exchange deerskins estimated at a total of 100,000 annually.[5] The river system could, of course, be used in this trade. In addition to this advantage, Charleston was 425 miles distant whereas Mobile was only 180.

As significant as were the geographical and economic potentialities of the site, the possibility of using it as a diplomatic post among the Indians of the area could be equally decisive in the contest. The success of the new colony of Louisiana, which was sparsely settled by whites, depended upon the ability to win the red men as allies or as benevolent neutrals. Agents were sent to the councils of the Indians to make treaties and alliances with them, and often Indian chiefs went to the posts to go through elaborate ceremonies of friendship and to secure presents. There was the keenest rivalry for the friendship of the Indians.

The four Indian groups in the area were the Choctaws, Chickasaws, Cherokees, and Creeks. The Choctaws were the Indians nearest the French, and their country extended north of Mobile, covering what is now most of western Alabama and southern and central Mississippi to the Mississippi River. The relations between the French and the Choctaws remained friendly during most of the French occupation. The Chickasaws occupied the country above the Choctaws in what is now northern Mississippi and western Tennessee. Although closer to the French in Louisiana than to the English in Carolina, the Chickasaws were generally to be found on the side of the English. The Cherokees lived between the Chickasaws and the English of Carolina, occupying what is now eastern Tennessee, western portions of the Carolinas and northern Alabama and Georgia. They were closer to Carolina and were usually found in the British camp, although there were noteworthy exceptions. Occupying much of the area between the English of Carolina and the French of eastern Louisiana, the Creeks lived in what is now central and southeastern Alabama and across the Chattahoochee in Georgia. These were said by James Adair to be the most powerful and to hold the "Indian balance of power in our southern parts,"[6] and he was the principal British contemporary authority on the natives. This was one point on which he and his French counterparts could agree.

The Upper Creeks occupied the area around the junction of the Coosa and Tallapoosa and up each stream. The Alabamas were the southernmost group of the Upper Creeks. Having villages in and around the peninsula formed by the rivers, they held a key position along the natural route between many of the other Upper and the Lower Creeks to the east. This is one reason why they held the balance of power among these Indians, exerting an influence far beyond their numbers. As long as the Alabamas remained neutral in the Franco-British rivalry, this most strategic geographical area would not be in hostile hands, and the French would have a degree of security. If French soldiers, agents, traders, and priests would use this advanced site as a base and could turn the Creeks and Cherokees against the English, the southern colonies of Britain would be in grave danger.

If the Alabamas were to espouse the French cause, or even to become neutral, however, there would have to be a revolutionary change in their attitude. The Creeks generally had been unfriendly to the French and the Alabamas had been particularly hostile. Shortly after Fort Louis de la Mobile was founded, the Alabamas showed their hostility. Thereupon, two expeditions were led against them by Jean Baptiste Lemoine de Bienville, younger brother of Iberville, who would eventually become the outstanding governor of Louisiana. Both expeditions failed, and the Alabamas in turn formed an Indian alliance in 1708 and threatened a great expedition against Mobile. Bienville offered a gun and five pounds of powder and ball for each Alabama scalp and the war dragged on for several years.[7]

In the winter of 1712-13, the Alabamas were reported by a Canadian who had been held prisoner there to have 300 dug-out canoes readied for descent against Mobile, and Bienville reported: "They can come down here in five days."[8] As late as the spring of 1715, the English still had trading posts in these villages and it was reported that the Alabamas were receiving muskets, balls, and powder and were ready to receive English carpenters and soldiers who would construct a fort and build flatboats which, loaded with Indians, would descend on Mobile.[9]

Naturally, the French were in their turn striving to win the Indians to their side. In this, they would be aided by certain fortuitous events which would enable them, rather than the English, to construct such a fort in the Alabama country.

II. *Conditions and Events Leading to the Establishment of the Post*

> This post appears to be absolutely necessary in
> order to bring the savages into the interest of the
> French. (Minutes of the Council of Marine, Paris,
> Sept. 8, 1716.)

One reason for the bleak prospects of the struggling French
settlements on the Gulf had been the war known as the War of the
Spanish Succession in Europe and as Queen Anne's War in America,
1702-13. Louis XIV had concentrated his efforts on the Continent,
and the British had the advantage at sea and in the colonies. In
addition to reports of impending British and Indian aggression by
land, there were rumors of attack by an English fleet. Little wonder
that the Mobilians were startled and, no doubt frightened, in the
early summer of 1713 when a fifty gun ship sailed up the bay with
cannons booming. But concern turned to joy when she proved to
be French and the bearer of good tidings: The war was over, and
there were new policies and promising plans for the colony. The
wealthy Antoine Crozat and his Company of Louisiana had been
made proprietor of Louisiana with the right to control and promote
trade and establish posts; in turn, the Company was required to
recruit colonists and furnish supplies. The new plans were to be
executed by an experienced colonial official who had been appointed
governor.[1]

He was Antoine de Lamothe Cadillac who had served well in
Canada. But his imperious and antagonistic nature did not endear
him to the natives of the American forest any more than to most of
his colleagues. In fact, his savage contemporaries in Louisiana rejected his haughty advances and his French critics would eventually
have him confined for a time in the Bastille after his recall to Paris.
He soon offended Bienville[2] to such an extent that the latter considered the possibility of demanding satisfaction on the field of honor!

Bienville himself was not slow to accept a quarrel and vicious
bickering among officials was almost continuous during Cadillac's
period of service[3] as well as during much of the history of the colony.

One of the many differences of opinion was the advisability of
establishing a post well above Mobile. Several new posts including
this one were authorized in 1714, but men and supplies were not

sufficient for all of them. As a consequence, Cadillac preferred to send the few available troops to new posts on the Mississippi. Bienville acknowledged that a fort on a distant frontier could exist only as long as the Indians in the region were friendly,[4] but he urged the establishment of one above Mobile in an effort to attach the Creeks to the French cause. While the governor was on a long voyage to the Illinois country in the spring of 1715, Bienville noticed that the Alabamas had stepped up their trade with the French. Thereupon, he decided to send agents to their villages.[5]

There must not have been time for the arrival of the agents before there began in April, 1715, a general rebellion against the grasping English traders and the expanding frontier settlements of Carolina.[6] This is known as the Yamasee War of 1715-16. It proved to be a serious if temporary blow to English trade and westward expansion. The Creeks probably initiated the conspiracy.[7] and they were to be the last to lay down their arms. In the autumn the Upper Creeks sent a delegation of chiefs to Fort Louis to ask the French for an alliance and to send traders to their country to replace the British. This could mean, it was estimated, the acquisition of 100,000 deerskins a year.[8]

The Yamasee War was a rare opportunity for the French. Fortunately for them, Cadillac was still on the lengthy mission up the Mississippi and Bienville was in command. This Metternich of the forest realized that the Creeks held the balance of power. They were more aggressive warriors, were more determined and successful hunters, and had used larger quantities of the white man's goods than more indolent tribes such as the Cherokees.[9] Bienville recognized also that, among the Creeks, it was the Alabamas who "must be won over to the French cause;" he had "essential genius for forest diplomacy" and would be equal to the occasion.[10] He readily promised to send French traders to their country to replace the British.[11] "The key to the Creek country and the most valuable strategic possession on the Carolina-Louisiana border was within French grasp."[12]

Astonishing as it may seem, the French came perilously close to missing the opportunity. Upon Cadillac's return, he still opposed the establishment of a fort above Mobile. One new argument was that a post established so soon after the uprising would cause the French to be blamed for instigating the massacre, an accusation which was already being made. Another was that he still did not trust such new-found allies as the Creeks.[13] There were only sixty soldiers for the three posts under consideration. Two of these were up the Mississippi — at the Natchez villages and at the mouth of the Wabash. The third was up the Alabama. The council of local officers considered the matter, and, according to Cadillac, the majority favored his proposal of postponing the establishment of the Wabash and Alabama posts in favor of the Natchez fort.[14]

According to Bienville, the majority favored his proposal and that of the Ordonnateur Duclos

> to make the establishment on the upper part of the river of the Alabamas in order to prevent the English from regaining the alliance with the Indians by means of a good trade that we should carry on at this fort so that all the nations hitherto in alliance with the English might find the same advantage with us that they had with the English, and to put in it the garrison of forty men as the Court had ordered and to postpone for that purpose the establishment of St. Jerome until we had here the thirty-five soldiers that his majesty had assigned to it, . . .

At any rate, the very next day, Cadillac ordered Bienville to prepare to depart for the Natchez to construct Fort Rosalie![15]

On two occasions within the next several months, there were reports that the English had won back the Alabamas who were about to lead an attack on Mobile. These proved to be false reports, but they strengthened the supporters of the Alabama post.[16]

Although the rumors that the British had regained their influence were inaccurate, the Carolinians did make a serious effort to recoup their losses as soon as the Yamassee War ended. In an effort to prevent unscrupulous traders from again bringing enraged savages down upon their settlements, a law was passed in June, 1716, establishing the strictest control over Indian trade. It was to be a public monopoly managed "for the sole Use, Benefit and Behoof of the Publick . . ." A board of commissioners was empowered to establish "factories" or trading posts and appoint "factors" with the sole right to trade with the Redmen.[17] Soon there came a resumption of trade with the Cherokees. Then, the Creeks sought peace and trade once again with the Carolinians.[18] Whatever the motives of the Creeks in the rapprochement with the English — whether they were tired of the procrastination of the French or were playing Hanoverian off against Bourbon at which they were skillful — the maneuver was successful. Colonel Theophilus Hastings, the Principal Factor for the Cherokee Trade, was granted a leave from his post in order to proceed to the Creek nation. This was on June 17, 1717.[19] This "extraordinary peace mission" included the veteran trader, John Musgrove and eight or ten others. Pack horses, supplies, and gifts were collected for the trip to the southwest to attach the Creeks to the English once again.[20]

In the meantime, the authorities in Paris had become more insistent on the establishment of a post among the Alabama Indians, even referring to it as "aux Alibamos" and "Post des Alibamons," and proposing that it consist of thirty men. "This post appears absolutely necessary" to "place the savages in our interest," Cadillac and Ordonnateur Duclos were notified in 1716. Major de Boisbriant was proposed as commandant and Lieutenant de la Tour as next in command.[21] In fact, Cadillac was recalled in the fall of 1716, and a more aggressive policy was adopted in Paris, though the authorities were still niggardly in furnishing men and supplies. His replacement, Governor de l'Epinay, arrived in the province in March of 1717. He soon asked Bienville to prepare a memoir on the establishments necessary in Louisiana, a statement which the latter supplied readily.[22]

When the new governor and the new ordonnateur, Hubert of St. Malo, studied the problem fully, they decided that the Alabama post appeared "the most urgent", and should be next. The two officials reported to the Council of Marine on May 30, 1717 that there were men and supplies for a detachment of only twenty, but "we are going to send it off". Boats were to be used, and "we are sending an interpreter with the detachment which is going to the Alabamas."[23]

The officer chosen to command the expedition and build the fort was Lieutenant de La Tour Vitral. He must have been a very spirited officer, though one of little distinction. He had been involved in incidents unbecoming an officer, at least in the opinion of Cadillac, and the Governor had him under suspension[24] at the time he was first being considered for the mission.[25]

At long last, the expedition set out. The Alabama post would be the second inland fort established in Louisiana. The expedition passed up the Mobile River to the confluence of the Tombigbee and the Alabama, went up the latter passing the present sites of Selma and Montgomery, and reached the heart of the Alabama country.

Thus both the French and the British sent rival expeditions to the area in the summer of 1717. The followers of the *Fleur de Lis*, led by Lieutenant La Tour, were the larger in size; going by boat, they planned to establish a frontier fort. The men carrying the Union Jack, led by Colonel Hastings, included a smaller number of troops; traveling in a pack train, their mission was to make peace with the natives, attach them to the English, and to reopen trade. If a clear-cut victory in the contest were won by either side, the whole of the southwest might be the eventual prize.

III. *The Construction of Fort Toulouse in 1717*

"If I had arrived one month later . . . the English would have won the [Creek] country." Lieutenant La Tour to Ordonnateur Hubert.

It was late in July when La Tour and his men reached their destination.[1] No doubt they explored the upper reaches of the Alabama and some distance up Coosa, if not the smaller Tallapoosa, looking for the best location. The site chosen was then four miles up the Coosa and on the east bank. That stream is navigable for several miles before reaching the fall line at what is now Wetumpka, and it has long navigable stretches as far upstream as Rome, Georgia. The river bank is unusually high here and the Tallapoosa bends to within five hundred yards, only to diverge again. This provided an ideal site. It dominated both streams. Furthermore, it was in the neck of a fairly large and level peninsular which was rich in soil, rich in fish, high enough at the site to be safe from floods, and well-drained.

No detailed plan of the fort has yet been found, but descriptions indicate it was in the pattern of the other frontier forts of the time. There was a stockade of logs enclosing an area of about one hundred yards square with a bastion at each corner.[2] It was probable that the logs were of oak, close to a foot in diameter and nine feet in length, and that the logs were stripped of bark, were charred for the three feet which were underground — at least this was the way the stockade was replaced in 1734. The logs were held together with laths which were nailed to them.[3] There were probably three gates to the fort. A moat was dug around the stockade, as deep as it was wide. Inside, there were frame buildings which served as offices and quarters for the garrison. Apparently there was also a watchtower in the center of the side opposite the river. The *magazin* was of masonry, no doubt of brick. It housed the precious powder, balls, guns, and supplies of all types. The powder *magazin* at Tombecbe, a companion fort, measured twenty-two by fourteen feet, was vaulted and covered with shingles. One or two iron cannon were placed in each bastion.

The new post was named Fort Toulouse in honor of Admiral Louis Alexandre de Bourbon, the Count of Toulouse who was the dominant member of the Council of Marine. This small group performed the function of secretary or minister of the navy and of colonies from 1715 to 1718. He was the legitimized son of Louis XIV[4] and Madame de Montespan, which explains the Bourbon in his name, and the County of Toulouse was one of the best known provinces in southern France. His frequent signature and initials found on numerous minutes of the Council which dealt with the establishment of the post, indicate the methodical care to administrative affairs for which he was noted.[5]

It was customary, however, for the French to use the name of the location of a fort more often than the official name. They referred to the post usually as the "Post aux Alibamons," or "Fort des Alibamons." On a few occasions, it was called "Fort Toulouse des Alibamons," and not infrequently the French referred to it simply as "aux Alibamons." The English usually called it the Alabama Fort or Post. In these two languages, it is probable that two dozen variations for its spelling by contemporaries can be found in the records.

With all of the documentation on the establishment of Fort Toulouse in 1717, it is surprising how persistently the date of 1714 continues in popular accounts. Perhaps this is because the construction was definitely proposed in 1714, and some contemporary accounts mistakenly gave that date, and because Albert J. Pickett's early and popular *History of Alabama* (Sheffield, Ala., 1896) also cited it.[6]

Pierre Heinrich used the French records to show the correct date in a volume printed as early as 1908,[7] but the volume was published in Paris and attracted little attention. Crane in his *Southern Frontier*, published in 1928, gave the correct date; A. B. Moore's *History of Alabama* has had it in all the editions published for a generation.[8]

The post should never be thought of as a fort against the Alabama Indians. It has been shown that the natives invited the French to their area during the Yamasee War against the English. It is obvious that they wanted the French as protectors and to secure from them European goods formerly sold by the traders from Charleston. There was one Alabama village "a musket shot" from the fort, another not much further from the stockade, and several other villages were within a few miles. A successful surprise attack by them would have been easy. It was expected that this and other such establishments would have an armorer to repair the guns of the chief Indians, and to do so without charge, so as to hold them to the French.[9] Some of the principal items among gifts and in trading were guns, powder, and balls. It was common knowledge that distant posts such as this one could exist only so long as the neighboring Indians were friendly or at least neutral. The handful of French soldiers were not expected to be able to defend it against the many Indians in the area. This would be recognized by the English in 1763 when they did find the Indians hostile in attitude and hence did not garrison the fort. The role of the fort was recognized about 1740 when the laconic comment was made that at this fort, "there is only a garrison for conserving the peace."[10] It was an establishment among the natives who were either allies or neutrals and it could serve as a significant military establishment only if the local Indians supported the French. It was a military base in that it was directed toward the English on one hand and on the other toward more distant Indians who might be unfriendly.

The Indians in the area were relatively numerous. Starting several miles above the post, Abihka, also known as Coosa, villages were scattered on both sides of the Coosa River. These were sometimes said to number about a dozen and to have twelve to fifteen hundred warriors, although the estimated number would vary considerably. The Tallapoosa villages started several miles to the east of the fort on the banks of the river of that name, and these were almost as numerous as the Abihkas. The Cowetas lived some sixty miles to the east and southeast on the Chattahoochee River. These were Lower Creeks. Sometimes the Alabamas tried to claim a sort of sovereignty among these other Creeks, but the usual estimate of their strength was only about four hundred men in half a dozen villages. There was much confusion concerning the numbers of the natives and relations between the Indian groups. Sometimes all the Creeks were called Alabamas by the French. The numerous Cherokees lived far to the northeast, the Choctaws to the southwest, and the Chickasaws to the northwest.

Thus the French at last occupied the strategic forks of the rivers. It was not a month too soon, for the English arrived late in August. Seeking to regain the friendship of the natives, the extraordinary peace and commercial mission despatched from Carolina had pushed west to the Tallapoosa near the river junction.[11] It was probably at Tukabatchee, just two leagues from the budding fort, that the British, said to be led by two officers and to number thirteen, encountered French traders on August 26. The latter were the Guenot de Trefontaine brothers who had been granted permits to trade about the time it was decided to construct the fort. The English had gifts for the Indians, as was customary when vying for Indian friendship, while Lieutenant de La Tour had none. The governor had violated the "code" by refusing to send any on this expedition. As a consequence, the Alabamas, even those in the village beside the fort site, made known their willingness to receive the British. Tension mounted. This threat called for emergency and immediate measures by the French. The lieutenant scraped up a few presents himself and the Trefontaines (who were afraid they might lose their goods anyway), agreed to the requisition of their merchandise to be used as presents. Except for these, "the English would have been received by this nation and that would have tended to the destruction of this colony," wrote Hubert the commissary general or ordonnateur.[12] From the new fort, La Tour himself reported "If I had arrived one month later I should not have been able to establish myself here because the English would have won the country" of the Creeks. As it was, he continued, the English "came close" to winning the Alabamas over to their side when they arrived with presents, while he had not been provided with them and this was made to look like a petty chief.[13] As it was, Governor L'Epinay still refused to send presents to the post,[14] although he had gifts which he himself distributed at the seat of government. The Carolinians were able to re-establish trade with Abihkas and many of the Tallapoosas soon after the new post was founded.[15] The French were still in possession of their new post; but the question was, could they hold it, now that their rivals had rallied and were *persona grata* to most of the Creeks?

It is difficult to resist a comparison of the race of the colonial rivals for the head of the Alabama River with that for the head of the Ohio in 1752-55.* The English reached the site of Pittsburgh, the junction of the Allegheny and Monongahela rivers, first and had begun their stockade fort early in 1754. The arrival of a larger French force two months later brought their surrender. The efforts to regain the strategic area helped lead to the French and Indian War, soon to become the Seven Years War. This would be a major contest fought on three continents, and would determine the supremacy in the North American continent. But in 1717, the English saw the French occupy the junction of Coosa and Tallapoosa rivers, which had once been under their influence. Would the British refrain from overt acts to reestablish their influence in the southern area?

IV. *Its Military Role and History to 1750*

"The post in the Alabamas, as is well-known, is one of the principal keys of His Majesty's domains on this continent." Governor Kerlerec in a *proces verbal* of May 16, 1760.[1]

The military history of the new post is best understood if the position it occupied in the colonial government and administration is comprehended. Canada was the older French province, and Britain had hopes of limiting it to the Great Lakes and St. Lawrence areas. The Carolinians had pushed their trade west to the lower Mississippi valley during the seventeenth century. When Louisiana settlements began at the turn of the century, the new French colony claimed the Illinois country, the Mississippi valley, and the Gulf area to the vicinity of Spanish Pensacola. France and England never did agree upon the boundaries between their empires. In fact, an agreement might limit opportunities for future expansion. Both claimed the entire area about the Fort Toulouse, but in their private correspondence, French officials acknowledged that the fort marked the easternmost boundary of Louisiana.[2]

When Louis XIV established the new colony, it, like the others,

came under the jurisdiction of the Ministry of Marine and Colonies.
Louisiana was first a royal colony, but in 1712 Antoine Crozat became the proprietor. The construction of the Alabama post was
seriously considered under his regime, but he relinquished the colony
in January, 1717. Construction of the fort was started while the
colony was a royal province again, but in August Louisiana was
granted to the Company of the West which the fabulous John Law
soon changed to the Company of the Indies. The more familiar
name was the Mississippi Company and there soon followed the
extravagant, even fanatical speculation in its stock which came to
a peak in the "Mississippi Bubble," only to burst in 1720. However,
the Company continued until 1731 when Louisiana became a royal
colony once again.

In practice, there was not much difference in the government
of the colony, whether royal or proprietary. The organization was
similar, and the colonial officials nominated by the directors of the
Company were always subject to the approval of the crown. Little
initiative was left to provincial officials and strict regulation of trade
under the Mercantilist theory was attempted. There were two principal officials in the colony who were of almost equal authority in
a kind of check and balance system. One was the "Governor" or
when that title was not used, "Commandant General". The other
was "Commissaire-Ordonnateur" or "Commissary General".

The governor had control over the armed forces, fortifications,
Indian. and related affairs. The *ordonnateur* had the authority of
an intendant; that is, he had jurisdiction over such matters as the
funds, provisions, control of the *magazins* or storehouses, and administration of justice. There was joint authority over the police.
land grants, commerce, and agriculture, but the line of demarcation
was not clear. If there were differences — and they were innumerable — they were to be referred to Versailles for solution. Each
could appeal directly and confidentially to the minister who acted
for the monarch. In the first years of his reign, Louis XV was a
minor. while in his later years matters of state bored him. One
of the infrequent ships carrying communications to France would
require about three months for a trip, so communication was slow.
There was a superior council of ranking officers which sometimes
exercised wide powers. Also, there were other councils which contested the authority of individual officials. Theoretically, the officers
in Louisiana were subordinate to those of Canada (or New France)

although not in practice. Lesser local officials sometimes claimed
jurisdiction over matters usually considered to be the prerogative
of the governor. Little wonder that Cadillac in his exasperation
wrote the minister "Decidedly, this colony is a monster without
head or tail, and its government is a shapeless absurdity. Verily,
I do not believe that there is in the whole universe such another
government."[3] Certainly, one should expect inefficiency, delay, and
indecision in handling governmental affairs.

The seat of government was moved from Mobile to Biloxi from
1720-22 and to New Orleans in the latter date. The outposts at
Mobile, the Alabamas, and Biloxi had now given a sufficient degree
of security for New Orleans to become a major establishment. It
had been founded in 1718, and ambitious development and construction were started in 1722, the year it became the provincial capital.
The best-known governors were Bienville who was in command
for four different terms, the Marquis de Vaudreuil, 1743-53, and
Sieur de Kerlerec, 1753-63. In 1721 the area around Fort Toulouse
become one of nine military-judiciary districts. This Alabama District
extended up the Alabama River as far as establishments were made.
Each district had its own commandant and judge. The Mobile and
Alabama districts had a joint commander. The other districts were
Biloxi, New Orleans, Natchitoches, Natchez, Yazoo, Arkansas, and
Illinois.[4]

It has been shown that the fort was not directed against the
Alabama Indians but against the English and more distant Indians
who might become unfriendly. No instance of the use of military
force against the Alabamas has been discovered. Direct threats
to use force seem to have been rare, also. Only one such instance
has been found. That was in 1748, when most of these Indians
were inclined to join in an expedition to force the Choctaws back
into line, but when some of the young men were anti-French in their
attitude. The latter had voiced for some time the idea that the
Alabamas should storm the fort and kill the garrison. Captain
Le Sueur met the threat by calling in the chiefs and assuring them
of French goodwill but promising that heads would fall if they laid
a hand on the French.[5]

The posts established in Louisiana by 1725 with an estimate of
the size of garrison needed in each were: Alabama with 15 men;
Mobile which was an important post, usually two companies or about

75 men; Dauphin Island, which protected Mobile on the approach by sea, only 7 men. Biloxi, protecting communications between Mobile and New Orleans, 7 men; The Balize, guarding the entrance to the Mississippi, a company of 35 or 40; Natchez, near the antagonistic Chickasaws, about 60 men; Yazoos, upstream, a garrison of 15; Arkansas, another post helping to protect convoys on the river, 8 men; Illinois still further upstream, a full company; Natchitoches, on the Red River, about 15 men; Fort Orleans on the Missouri, 12 soldiers,[6] and New Orleans with the largest garrison, four companies by 1734. In fact, the number of men in garrisons had increased somewhat by the later date with thirty men at the Alabamas.[7] Although Iberville's plan of a ring of forts around the English colonies, each within a day's travel of the other, was not realized, these posts, with the establishments in Canada, did surround the area claimed by the British colonies.

Within the next decades, two significant wars would be fought with the eastern half of North America, if not the whole continent as a prize. But in the area around the Alabama post, there was always at least a "cold war" going on between the principal rivals. France and Britain both claimed the area about the fort. At times, it was a triangular rivalry which included the Spanish of Florida. Usually, however, the relations between the French and the latter were amicable. Governor John Barnwell of South Carolina was among those who realized the threat posed by the Alabama post. He proposed the construction of English forts on the Chattahoochee and the Alabama or Tennessee in 1720 and other proposals were made from time to time.[8] South Carolina's council voted in 1727 to build a fort in the Upper Creek country at Okfuskee.[9] This location is approximately thirty-five miles up the Tallapoosa and to the west of the present town of Dadeville.[10] But no fort was built there at this or any other time. There does appear to have been an English military outpost of sorts there, and various writers have concluded that it was an English fort. No fort, as a matter of fact, was ever established in the vicinity of the Alabamas, though forts were built in the Cherokee country. But British traders usually lived in the major Creek towns (other than Alabama towns); English agents accompanied by military personnel were sent to the Creeks from time to time; occasionally, officials paid visits to their chiefs; and presents were distributed by English agents and officers in order to gain native support.

The Toulouse post also had its officers and men, traders, and sometimes missionaries, all seeking to control the natives. They, too, distributed presents. Most of the redmen saw their opportunity and played one group of whites against the other. Each of the latter was positive that the other was distributing many more presents among the Indians and had greater government support in this contest for Indian allies. Each of the European powers knew that if the other could exert sufficient influence over the natives, it could drive its rival out of the vast borderland. In peace time, Europeans did not usually shed the blood of Europeans or incite the Indians to murder, but property was far from inviolate. It was common practice to pay the redmen for Indian scalps and slaves from unfriendly tribes.[11] One move in the international rivalry was the establishment of the colony of Georgia in 1733. One of the major reasons for the new colony was to bolster the frontier against the Spaniards and French and to occupy more of the land in dispute.[12] Thus the establishment and success of Fort Toulouse contributed to the decision to establish Georgia. Under these conditions there were frequent rumors of wars and two major wars would occur.

If the Fort Toulouse garrison should be called on to engage in hostilities, how well-prepared would it be? Colonial military organizations — whether British, Spanish, or French — were known to be inefficient with garrisons undisciplined and ineffective by European standards. Assignments to service in French colonies sometimes came as punishment for infractions by soldiers in the mother country. Commissions were granted on the basis of family rank and it was not unusual for intractable sons in noble families to be given commissions in the colonial service. Commandants at the Louisiana posts frequently showed too much interest in profits made in trading with the natives, even when this was expressly forbidden, and too little zeal in military matters. The very organization of the government contributed to the quarreling and bickering among officers. A chronic shortage of provisions, even food, poor living quarters, and the dullness of life on each of the posts contributed to the lack of discipline among the men.

Even by these standards, the Alabama post was a special problem. It was one of the "distant" posts and supplies were slow in arriving from the coast, the quarters were usually in need of repair, and garrison duty deep in the forest borderland was especially dull. Furthermore, the English were a continual threat in one way and a temptation in another. Traders and agents of this nationality were frequently only a few miles distant from the garrison and might succeed at any moment in persuading the Creeks to attack the French fort. It was a common belief they were buying the red man's good will by selling goods at much lower prices and by distributing fabulous quantities of gifts to the chief warriors. The Indians helped, of course, to encourage these exaggerated ideas as to prices and gifts. At the same time, discontented men were tempted to go over to the British to escape military duty and perhaps to work their way to the Atlantic coast. It was recognized by the Louisiana officials that "disorders have happened there [Fort Toulouse] more frequently than elsewhere" and "that extreme consideration had always been given to this post" because of the special problems existing there.[13] Under these conditions there is little wonder that desertion was not unusual. In fact, there was a serious mutiny four years after its construction.

The traditional account[14] has it that the soldiers all arose against their officers and killed Commandant Marchand, but Ensign Villemerieu (sometimes written as Villemont) and a junior officer named Paque managed to escape. That the mutineers ransacked the fort, cooked and ate a hearty meal, took arms from the *magazin* and whatever else they wished, left the fort, crossed the Tallapoosa at what was later called Grey's Ferry, and headed for Carolina; that the younger officer went to the Indians for help—Villemerieu to Hickory Ground near Wetumpka and Paque to Coosada down the river; that the officers secured a new command, started in pursuit, and ambushed the mutineers; that sixteen of the men were killed in the desperate fighting, several were captured, and two escaped, that young Paque with an Indian guard soon took them to Mobile where they arrived on September 19, and that the men were later executed.[15]

Actually, the mutiny was sparked by three sergeants and five men from the Mobile garrison who deserted and fled to the Alabama post. Here, the deserters were able to persuade two-thirds of the garrison to mutiny. The total size of the garrison at the time was probably twenty-five to thirty men, including officers.[16] The mutineers seized and bound the officers on August 25 and set out for Carolina "with drums beating [and] fuses lighted." As they left, they unbound the officers. These turned to the Alabama Indians for aid, and the response was so rapid that within two hours 250

men were in pursuit. The latter overtook the deserters within thirty
miles and attacked and "killed eighteen of them on the spot;" the
remainder were captured and taken to the post to be court martialed.
The one sergeant who was captured was found guilty and condemned
"to be tomahawked immediately and all the others to be convicts
for life."[17]

There is no reason to believe that Marchand was killed in
the mutiny and buried by a Jesuit. The official account summarized
above expressly states that the officers were freed. Their names
were not given. As a matter of fact, an officer by the name of
Marchand may never have been in immediate command of the post;
at least the author has seen no official evidence that one was. A
Captain Marchand de Courcelle appears in the records frequently
and for a decade after the mutiny. He was stationed at Mobile for
some time, and it was his company from which the detachments
for the Alabama post were taken.[18] Perhaps the confusion concerning his position stems from the fact that in Mobile there was a
supervisor of the Alabama district known as "Commandant aux Alibamons." Marchand held this position for some years. Missionaries
had not been stationed there this early in the history of the post,
nor had the officer in command ever held as high a rank as Captain.

Four years later, it was reported that another group deserted
to the English.[19] While desertion was not unusual in the various
posts of Louisiana, it does appear to have been more extensive in
this post which was in such close proximity to the British. Sometimes they were returned by friendly Indians. Two deserters, for
example, were returned to the post in 1737 on condition that their
lives be spared. This put the authorities of Louisiana in a difficult
position, being caught between the dilemma of keeping their word
with the red men and abiding by French law.[20]

Recognizing the problem of discipline, a special effort was made
to pick the best officers and men for the more distant posts. Pressure
for this was exerted in Paris from time to time,[21] and the governors
sought to have reliable officers and men picked for the distant
posts.[22] When Governor Perier de Salvert gave Commandant Diron
a severe dressing down in 1729 and ordered him to select with
more care the men destined for the Alabama garrison, to increase
its size, and to eliminate the causes for the desertions there,[23] the
Mobile officer responded in frank terms. He would increase the

provisions when he had sufficient supplies. As for despatching additional men from the Mobile garrison, those who had been there any length of time had adapted themselves to that post and usually had families and would be loath to abandon their homes. Only the untried newcomers were left from which to choose men for the outpost.[24] Rotation, which would shorten the assignment to this and three other posts, was proposed by Bienville in 1733,[25] but desertions at the various posts continued.

The famed Swiss mercenaries were used in the colony along with natives of France and they were better disciplined. Some governors frankly informed their superiors that these soldiers were preferred.

As for quality, the men in command at the post of the Alabamas appear to have been relatively good officers. The rank was usually that of lieutenant in the first decades and captain in the later years.[26]

The quality of the wooden stockade and frame buildings of the post was no doubt poor. They rotted quickly and the earthen ramparts eroded soon after they were put up. The constructions had to be repaired or rebuilt from time to time. The fort was less than four years old when it was declared to be in bad condition.[27] The curtains were renewed, but it was reported by La Tour to be in "very bad condition" and not safe from English and unfriendly Indians in 1723. He secured the approval of the Superior Council to repair the bastions and the buildings. The cost was estimated at 1,000 livres "in suitable merchandise," which was deemed to be "five *quarts*" (about 100 gallons) of brandy and twenty-six and two-thirds ells (approximately 50 yards) of limburg cloth.[28] It was common practice to use the barter system, and these were two of the commodities in greatest demand at the post. While La Tour was for maintaining it in good repair, at least one official in this period thought such expenditures were wasted and proposed that it be moved to a different location. He was Sieur de Pauger, an engineer and assistant to La Tour — and a critic of the latter. It appears that the expense for these repairs exceeded the estimate by about 60 per cent. Pauger thought there was nothing to do but pay the bill this time, but he proposed that the post should be moved far downstream to within 100 miles of Mobile where there was a quarry. There, a fort could be constructed which could be defended from the English and hostile Indians. If the existing site were not to be abandoned, perhaps an earth redoubt which would be cheaper to maintain could be constructed.[29]

His advice was not followed and Bienville and the ordonnateur found in 1733 that the stockade was "entirely destroyed." The governor ordered it to be rebuilt and the commander and *garde magazin* (keeper of the warehouse) contracted with some members of the garrison to reconstruct it. The soldiers agreed to use "oak piles three feet in circumference, without bark, by nine feet high of which the lower part that is to be placed in the ground shall be charred, all well trimmed and nailed, at the rate of one hundred and thirty livres for each hundred piles." The nails were supplied by the authorities, and the work was completed by 1736. The fort of the Natchitoches was to have a new stockade at the same time, but the piles were to be eleven feet in length.[30]

Again, in 1748 the works were reported as having rotted and the entire fort needed to be rebuilt. By this time, it had to be relocated, however. The fort was opposite a sharp bend in the river and the current ate into the bank. As a report of 1748 put it, "the spot on which the fort is located" is "eaten away every day." A man with some engineering knowledge, one Saucier, was sent to the Alabama post in 1748 to consult with the commandant, Captain Le Sueur, and make recommendations. His report was forwarded to New Orleans,[31] and the fort was built anew in 1751.[32] It was in need of repairs once again by 1755.

It is difficult to determine the armament at the fort at various periods. When the Company of the Indies returned the colony to the Crown in 1731, the fort was said to contain two cannons, two cast-iron and the same number of iron mortars, and seven mortar-breeches.[33] There was some talk of placing French cavalry in the areas most exposed to the English. Also, there were proposals that some *coureurs de bois* be brought down from Canada to the Alabama and other inland posts to strengthen the barrier against the British.[34] No evidence has been found that these were carried out at Fort Toulouse.

Undoubtedly, the fort was very lightly armed, both by European and by coastal standards. But it was a frontier post, and these were usually small. If the Alabamas and other Creeks proved loyal to the garrison, it was a military establishment to be reckoned with.

An illustration of the use it could be to the French even in time of peace occurred in 1735. The British had the audacity to attempt to set up a trading post at "Akouitamopa," an Alabama town just "one league from our fort," as Bienville expressed it. Two Englishmen, accompanied by some Alabama chiefs made the effort. Whereupon, Lieutenant Benoist, who was in command of the fort, led eight soldiers and several prominent Alabamas to the village. In the words of Bienville again, he "obliged these English to retire."[35]

Although not a large post, it was one which the English feared. Within a year after its construction in 1717, the Charlestown authorities had a report from Colonel Hastings that the French were inciting the Creeks to attack the friendly Cherokees, and might even lead the Indians in the attack. The threat was taken so seriously that fifty men were ordered to the Congarees; if any Frenchmen were with the Creeks, the English soldiers were to lead the Cherokees in an advance against them.[36] James Adair's favorite term in referring to it was the "dangerous Alebahma" fort. He was familiar with the fort and considered it to be "directed by skillful officers" and to be "supplied pretty well" with presents for the Indians.[37] Lachlan McGillivray, who was living among the Upper Creeks when it was rebuilt in 1751, reported that it was a "pretty strong" one.[38]

The first formal war involving the post directly, however, was King George's War between Britain and France, 1744-48. For several years previously, there was fighting between the English and Spanish colonies as well as in Europe, and the entire war is known as the War of the Austrian Succession, 1740-48. The fighting between the southern English colonies and the Spanish of Florida was on a large scale. Naturally, there were numerous reports of impending war. As early as 1735, the Minister and Bienville were in agreement that if war with the English came, Louisiana would have nothing to fear except the interruption of trade — and at the frontier post of Fort Toulouse. They agreed that the "establishment des Alibamons" would be the one which would be in greatest danger. All possible measures would be taken to place the interior of the colony in security, the Minister, Count de Maurepas, instructed Bienville; furthermore, the colonial official should neglect nothing in his efforts to maintain the savages in the Alabama region in the interests of France.[39]

When King George's War did break out, however, Governor James Glen of South Carolina had a plan for a concerted effort against Louisiana. He proposed to attack both in the Alabama country (using the Creeks and building a strong fort in their country) and on the coast.[40] No such expeditions were despatched, but rumors of impending attacks reached the colony and mother country and additional arms and men were despatched to the colony. In this period, the Alabama fort was strengthened somewhat, being increased to a garrison approaching fifty men.

The English settlers likewise heard rumors of French plans to attack. They were alarmed annually over reports of plans to subvert the slaves, rally friendly Indians, and march against Georgia and the Carolinas. Governor Glen realized that the rumors placed more men in the French invading forces than were in the entire colony; but he did acknowledge that the Louisiana rivals might find it easy to use Indians in an attack and that "the French fort called the Alabamas which I have so frequently mentioned" was "an Eyesore" to his province. He proposed the construction of four British forts in the frontier area ranging in garrisons from twenty-five to 100 men, but none was proposed adjacent to the Alabama country,[41] and none of the proposed forts was constructed at this time. The war ended with the Treaty of Aix-la-Chapelle, 1748, without a hostile shot having been fired from the stockade of Fort Toulouse — at least as far as is known. In fact, there were no hostilities involving Louisiana. The treaty brought only an uneasy truce, both in America and in Europe. The fighting which would grow into the French and Indian War would begin within six years.

This war, known in Europe as the Seven Years' War, 1756-63, would prove to be a showdown between Briton and Gaul. The stakes in this continent would be the English Thirteen Colonies and French Canada and Louisiana. Before examining the outcome of this final contest, what were the non-military activities at the fort, and what sort of everyday life was led on the post?

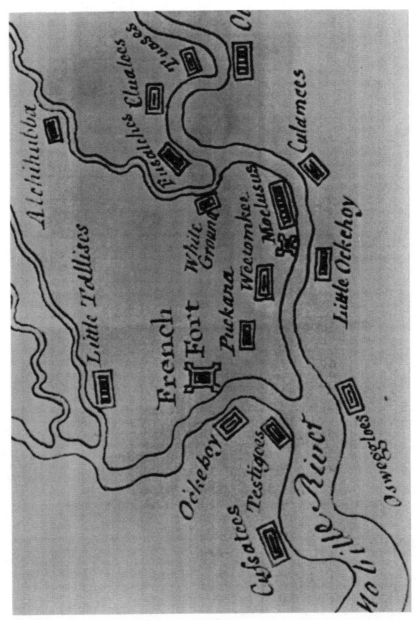

A detail of "A Draught of the Upper Creek Nation," 1757. (Sir Thomas Gage Papers, courtesy of the William L. Clement Library, University of Michigan).

V. *Life on the Post*

> Typical nicknames of men in the garrison: Mathieu
> "Jolly" Brignac, Louis "Debonair" Fonteneau, Pierre
> "Richelieu" Fourre, St. Simeon "St. Peter" Brignac,
> Simeon "Carefree" Dousset, Joseph "Hurricane" Cev-
> raise, Antoine "from Dauphine" Bonin. (From the
> Review of the Garrison, January 1, 1756.)

One of the most difficult tasks of the historian is the description
of the everyday life, of the daily activities of ordinary people, of a
past generation. As for the history of Fort Toulouse, the records
on the major events and personalities are numerous, but those on
ordinary men and activities are scarce. Scanty though these particular sources may be, some idea of garrison life can be gained.

One of the events which must have enlivened the tedium of
garrison duty was the arrival of boats from Mobile. They were
used to send not only men and mail to the post of the Alabamas, but
also clothes, ammunition, some food, various other supplies for the
garrison, goods for barter with the Indians, — and of course news.[1]
The boats would contain an escort of a sargeant and, when possible to
spare them, four men.[2] They were fairly large flat bottom boats
and were sometimes as much as forty feet long with a beam of
nine feet. These larger boats used twenty-four or twenty-eight
oarsmen and could carry forty tons. Others were smaller, such as
twenty-five and sixteen ton boats, and used a smaller crew. They
were maintained at Mobile for service between this base and New
Orleans, Toulouse, and Tombecbe. Negro slaves were trained to
man them but were never sufficient in number; consequently, the
soldiers were used as oarsmen,[3] or Indians were employed. A boat
was also maintained at the post. One of the soldiers, Jean Brudel,
sometimes spelled Bradel and nicknamed "La Rose", became so
adept as master of the fort's boat that he was given a sizeable
increase in pay — 200 livres — and also eighteen *pots* of brandy per
year, or a little more than a pint for each Saturday night in the year.[4]

As a boat bound for the Alabamas reached its destination and
was rowed to starboard or the east bank of the Coosa, one could
see little of the post. The river bank is high and almost perpendicular
at this point, although upon closer observation there was seen to
be a ravine or gully which formed a natural ramp to the top. There,
the fort came into view. There would probably be little of the

traditional military "spit and polish" or of discipline to observe. The men were issued clothes and might wear a uniform on special occasions. But it is probable that the only man who regularly dressed in anything resembling a real uniform was the officer in charge, and his was not comparable to the stately and colorful ones prescribed for officers and probably worn on the important coastal posts.[5] Even at the latter, uniforms varied in material, if not otherwise.[6] There must have been a large degree of informality except in relations with the commander. One thing which would probably have seemed more "military" was the use of drums, for drummers appear to have been assigned to the garrison regularly.

Alabama Indians probably had free access to the vicinity of the stockade if not within. There appears to have been relatively good relations between members of the garrison and these natives.[7] Although Indians were known to overtake and return deserters, they would also intercede for them. There were cases in which the red skins would turn them in only under promise of leniency by the officer in charge.[8] Throughout its history, one Indian village appears to have been located just south of the fort. It was described as only a musket-shot or 150 yards distant and was usually known to the French as Pacana or Pakana. About the same distance to the east, there was usually another, sometimes called Tomopa or Tomapa.[9]

A few French civilians, who were Indian traders using the post as a base, might have been encountered within the stockade. For some years it is improbable that many, if any, settlers lived in the area. Civilians eventually did settle there, and soldiers were sometimes released from the service if they agreed to settle near their posts. By 1758 a census of the community showed over 160 inhabitants. There were two dozen families with children.[10] The average number of children in these families was four, so, by the 1750's the sound of children playing must have been commonplace around the fort[11] Permission was given for the members of the garrison to marry Indians in the hope that they might be less inclined to desert.

The lack of morality of this and other posts was deplored frequently, and gambling was high on the list of vices denounced by priests and authorities alike. It was so serious a problem that the Superior Council tried to curtail it in 1723. This body forbade the playing at home of any game of chance with stakes. Outside the home, it permitted "games of recreation" only, with stakes below 100 livres. All obligations to pay gambling debts above that sum were null and void and the fines for exceeding the limit were to go toward the support of the hospital in New Orleans.[12] If the author has interpreted this decree properly, it is the first time that he has seen an official line of demarcation between a game of chance for recreation only and illegal gambling — the figure of 100 livres! Very few men could gamble with money, for currency of all kinds was scarce in the whole colony and in inland posts in particular.

The paymaster, for the men, but apparently not for the commissioned officers, was the clerk, who was also the *garde magazin*, and who kept very exact and formal accounts of expenditures. They show that, about the time the fort was established, the official pay to soldiers in Louisiana was: Captains, 90 francs per month; lieutenants, 60; sergeants, 19 and 10 sols; corporals and drummers, 13 and 10; and fusiliers or privates, 9 francs. From this amount, there were deductions from the pay of non-commissioned officers and men: 3 francs for bread or grain for bread;[13] 2 francs and 5 sols for clothing (3 for sergeants); and 1 franc 10 sols for approximately one pound of powder. Thus the "take home" pay for a private would have been 2 livres five sols per month from which he would have had to pay for food other than bread,[14] except that the local authorities had paid an additional "cost of living bonus of 3 francs 5 sols before it was regularized by an ordinance. But "extreme consideration" was sometimes given to the Alabama garrison, so exposed, so near the English and so inclined to disorders. Therefore, higher pay was given to all but commissioned officers for service there for a time in its early history.[15] Barter was the means of exchange, so the men at the interior posts were paid in merchandise.

It is extremely difficult to determine the value or purchasing power of the pay received. Prices fluctuated considerably and varied from place to place, despite the effort to regulate prices. According to the official or legal prices in this early period, which were often lower than in practice, a quarter of a deer was worth 4 livres or about one-third of a month's pay of a private. A chicken was officially priced at 3 livres, so he might buy 3 or 4 with his month's pay. These were probably cheaper at the fort, however. Red wine was sold at the canteen in Biloxi, the capital, in 1722, at about a livre per quart and brandy about a livre per pint.[16] But a Fort Toulouse soldier usually took his pay in powder and balls, as did men at the other interior posts.[17] With these, he could shoot his own game and barter with Indians for skins or food, and with traders and the *garde magazin* for merchandise. Powder and balls were the common media of exchange. In addition to taking his pay in ammunition, he would sometimes take it in cloth, salt, vermillion, knives, or other commodities.[18]

The *commis garde magazin* (clerk of the records as well as warehouse or storehouse keeper) in 1721-22 was La Lande and he received a salary of 600 livres per year. This made him, along with the surgeon, the second highest paid among the personnel.[19] Surgeons, when available, were not always so well paid; nor were they well-trained. The first one at Fort Toulouse appears to have been a man named Vauthier with a salary of 600 livres per year, and the right to buy grain for his food.[20] But in 1729 another named Melizan was paid only 300 livres, which was much less than carpenters were paid in Louisiana. The salary then budgeted for the Alabama interpreter (and only 4 were listed for all of Louisiana) was 250. By this date, La Lande, who was said to have been especially capable as clerk and storehouse keeper, received in allowance and pay 1245 livres for this year.[21] In 1733 a young man named Gandeau served as surgeon, clerk and *garde magazin* at the post.[22]

Later, compensation for service in Louisiana increased somewhat, especially for the officers and civil employees, and deductions varied. Also, bonuses might be paid for special merit, but again these were usually to officers or skilled workers. Sometimes, also, a soldier would be allowed additional food if his wife lived in Louisiana.

The payrolls at the fort show the typical French names one would expect and, on some occasions, a clerk with time on his hands would add the nicknames after their names. Some of these may be translated as. "the Jolly", "the Debonair", "the Light-Hearted", "the Carefree", "the Hurricane". As might be expected, other soldiers were called "Richelieu", or "St. Louis", or the province from which they came.[23] There were several sons who volunteered to serve with their fathers in the latter years of the post.[24]

The amount of sickness among the troops of this post was at times abnormally high, especially in the early years. Lieutenant

La Tour and his sergeant were two of the first victims. The latter was so ill with diarrhea and fever that he was taken down to Mobile by a soldier and two Alabamas.[25] The officer stuck it out at the post, but reported at the end of the winter that for seven months he had lingered "between life and death" from dysentary.[26] The garrison had no physician. La Tour's plea for a surgeon to substitute for a physician, was not met at first. These, too, were scarce. When still other members of the garrison became ill the next year and some died, the first surgeon, Vauthier was assigned to the post.[27]

Health conditions appear to have improved somewhat in time, but a member of the military service did not have a good prospect of ever returning home. It was difficult to gain a transfer to France, or even to retire and return to France, although it was not so difficult to secure a separation from the service in order to settle in the colony. A "General Roll of Troops in Louisiana" from 1734 to 1771 gives the fate of a number of the men. It indicates a terrible rate of mortality for Louisiana troops. Many were listed as simply having died while in service, although Fort Toulouse does not have more than its share of these in this list. Quite a few men drowned, especially on the Mississippi, but only one name was so identified with the Alabama post. He was Etienne Verrier, drowned "while returning from the Alabamas" on October 1, 1759. A number were listed as having deserted, particularly in the last years of the colony. Although Fort Toulouse had its share and more of these during its history, only one was so identified in this list; he was an Antoine Vespy, and the date February 15, 1755. Perhaps desertions from this post declined in later years. Relatively few men were listed as killed by Indians — and only one member of the Alabama garrison was so listed. Still others were sent to the galleys or shot for desertion, but none was so listed from the Alabama post.[28]

If the health of the garrison were poor, especially in the early years, there is little wonder. It was up to each individual soldier to provide his own food. Much of the time, there was not even a mill to grind the grain which was supplied him. The Council at the capital, conscious of the suffering that resulted, decided to buy a hand-mill in March of 1719.[29] Something must have prevented this, or it must have broken down, for the fact that there was no mill at the Alabama post was one reason given for the mutiny of August 1721. The men were said to pay Indian women one-third of the

grain for grinding it, since their frequent guard and detachment
duty did not permit the time to grind it themselves.[30]

A shortage of provisions was a common complaint. Flour from
France or the other colonies was lacking on many occasions, especially during war, when the English controlled the sea lanes to
Louisiana. Rice was then added to the flour, much to the disgust
of the garrison.[31] Both rice and corn were sometimes added and
during part of the French and Indian war, corn alone was available.
By this time, however, the men were paid for having their own
corn, called *mahis,* ground.[32] On at least one occasion, the winter
of 1745-46, if not on others, the commanding officer was reduced
to the extremity of sending the men to the Indian villages for subsistence.[33] Furthermore, the troops were apparently not furnished
beds, mattresses, ticking, or blankets.[34] Little wonder that desertion
was common and mutiny might be imminent at any time. There was
consternation when an officer, Chevalier de Lantagnac, a second
ensign, disappeared and was presumed in 1747 to have deserted.[35]
He was quite young, however, and he returned eight years later
claiming that he had not deserted. He insisted that he had become
lost while hunting, that he had been forced by Chickasaws to ac-
company them to the English, that he had pretended to become
interested in trade with the Indians, that he used trips into the wilder-
ness as a means of learning the geography of the area, and that he
finally had been able to use a trading mission as a ruse to escape
and return to the Alabama post.[36]

French sou, a copper coin circulated in the Louisiana colony. This coin was
excavated at the site of Hoithlewaulee, a Creek Indian town situated about twelve
miles east of Fort Toulouse. (Photograph by Paula Weiss).

VI. *Trade at the Alabama Post*

> "The officers who had been at Tombeckbi and Ala-
> bama, Own'd to me, that they generally bought of
> the Indians about these places, fifty thousand skins
> a year, each." (Colonel Robertson to Major General
> Gage, March 8, 1764.)
> The number of pelts produced by the Alabamas in
> 1725 is estimated at 3,000. (Surrey, *Commerce of
> Louisiana.*)

The officials of Louisiana were not only interested in promoting
trade generally; frequently, the officers were themselves the principal
traders at the posts.[1] From time to time the home authorities complained of this and of the rapacious nature of the officers.[2] There
is no reason to believe the commanding officers at the Alabamas
were exceptions. Their participation in trade naturally discouraged
the civilian traders. The latter were required at one time to report
to the commanding officer upon arrival and to get permission to
leave a post during the early years of Fort Toulouse. When this
practice was forbidden, the officers still sought to exercise some
control over the traders; this, too, was forbidden by the colonial
authorities. Throughout the colonial period, the authorities attempted
to set prices,[3] and the regulations concerning trade with the Indians
were changed from time to time. French traders could secure goods
from the warehouses (provided their credit or securities were good),
trade with the Indians, and pay the debt at the fixed rate per pound
for peltries.[4]

Frenchmen trading with the Alabamas would usually take the
river route from Mobile, although some used the land route. The
latter joined the northern path from Pensacola. The fort was the
terminus of this trading path from the south.

Fort Toulouse also lay athwart the famed English Lower Path
to Charleston; in fact, it was located near the intersection of the
two branches of this Lower Path. One came from the northwest
and the Chickasaw lands and the other from the west and the Choctaw country. Meeting just below the fort, they formed a single route
to Charleston. It followed the Tallapoosa for some miles, then turned
due east to the Chattahoochee and then northeast. Near the Savannah river, it made a junction with the Upper Path. The latter started
at the Mississippi and moved east through the heart of the Chicka-

saw territory to the Coosa. There it veered southeast to the Tallapoosa, crossing this river about where Tallassee now stands. This
was twenty-five miles up the river from the fort. From there it led
due east and joined the Lower Path to form a single route, the main
one from the west and southwest to the well-stocked warehouses of
Charleston. The English traders and agents had used it for decades.[5]

Thus French traders using Fort Toulouse as a center could use
the four main paths — southwest to Mobile, west toward the Choctaws, northwest in the direction of the Chickasaws, and northeast
through the Creek areas. They preferred the waterways, however.

The English traders, on the other hand, used the paths primarily,
utilizing pack horses, drivers, slaves, and Indians. At first the individual Carolina trader was apt to employ one pack horse-man with
six or seven animals in covering the almost five hundred mile journey
from the Alabamas to Charleston in twenty-seven days or so. The
size of the caravan soon increased to three or four pack horse-men
and twenty to thirty horses. These were fine native animals which
could carry packs totalling 150 pounds each. Indian and slave
burdeners were expected to carry about thirty skins weighing perhaps fifty to sixty pounds. A periago rowed by seven or eight men
might hold 500 to 700 skins.[6] The pack trains moved in Indian file
along the paths.

> After the order of march for the day was arranged,
> the chief driver cracked his tough cowhide whip
> and gave an Indian whoop, both of which were re-
> peated by the other drivers, and at once the train
> set off at a brisk trot that was not slackened as long
> as the horses were able to move forward. . . . When
> two of the horse-trains met on the trail they saluted
> each other several times with a general whoop and
> other shouts of friendship. Then they struck camp
> near each other.[7]

When a stream could be forded, the men stripped, the horses were
driven across, and the men ferried their baggage. In other cases,
rafts were quickly built, a grapevine was tied to it, and a man swam
across with the end in his mouth and pulled the raft across. An
individual pack-peddler who made an Indian village his headquarters
might follow the natives on a hunting trip, holding his pack in place
by a head-band if he were French. He and the Indians would cross

streams by cutting down sapplings or trees and make a "raccoon bridge."[8]

The principal product the natives had for exchange was deer skins or, after they began to cure the skins, leather. They had fresh venison, of course, and tallow. They had some fowl and, at times, maize or corn.[9] The natives had an insatiable demand for guns, powder, and balls, for by 1725 the Creeks were relying heavily on guns when hunting. By this date they were accustomed also to axes and hoes instead of stone implements and the white man's cloth rather than skins for clothing.[10] The records of the garrison show that even during war, when the English blockade was stringent, the fort had powder, balls, flints, and salt.[11] It was generally conceded that the French powder and balls were superior to the British. The same could not be said for other products,[12] except perhaps brandy, and the brandy was often watered down. Bienville reported in 1737 that the Alabama traders made a high profit on brandy. He blamed the British for starting the traffic with the Creeks. Decrees were sometimes issued forbidding the sale of alcoholic beverages to the red men but the prohibition was not enforced.[13] The Carolinian officials made a strong effort to prevent commerce in rum when they began to trade again with the Creeks in 1717, but this was hard to prohibit. It is known that at times that their traders sold rum on credit.[14]

The garrison payrolls show that the men took their pay also in guns, ribbon, shirts, vermillion, salt, and *couteaux boucherons* which were woodmen's knives or axes.[15] Limburg cloth was a popular commodity in the trade at the post.[16] The post was also a center in such products as blankets, needles, razors, trinkets, scissors, mirrors, belts, shoes, hats, and shirts.[17]

The British had a greater variety of goods; also, their styles and designs were preferred by the Indians. The French sought to meet this competition for the Alabama trade. So strong was the French desire to please this group of red skins that Commander Hazeur requested that shoe buckles and earrings of the particular design preferred by them be manufactured especially for their trade in 1741. Bienville and Ordonnateur Salmon supported his recommendation and added a third item — ribbon. Samples of the styles of all three commodities were sent to France. The minister of colonies had French companies copy the sample and manufacture the commodities for the trade with the Alabamas. Hazeur was commended for his zeal in the matter — but, to his disappointment, it did not lead to an early promotion to Captain![18] This is another indication of the special consideration given to the Alabamas in the competition with the English for their trade, good will, and support.

At times French goods were sold to the Alabamas at prices lower than at other inland posts. In 1721, for example, the price for commodities at the Natchez and Yazoo posts was 70 per cent above the price in France and prices at more distant posts went as high as 100 per cent. The price at the Alabamas, however, was the same as at the ports, 50 per cent, "due to the necessity of making the price in this area as cheap as the English do."[19] In 1735 there was such competition for the good will and support of the Alabamas that the French went through the pretense of cutting French prices to meet English competition and did change the French method of computing the value of peltries.

This was when Lieutenant Benoit or Benoist was in command of the post and was in one of the periods in which the British were most daring and aggressive. It was one of the many times that the officer in command feared that the Alabamas might go over to the British, if the British prices were not met. Thereupon, Bienville agreed to abandon the French practice of giving prices simply in number of skins, regardless of weight. He agreed to adopt the English practice of classifying them into large skins (two pounds or more), medium (one and a quarter to two pounds), and small ones (less than a pound and a quarter). A large skin was worth two of medium size or three small ones. Thus "an ell and a half [between five and six feet] of limburg cloth, which here [New Orleans] costs the King twelve livres, will be sold for five large skins or ten medium-sized which at thirty sous a poud will bring at least fifteen livres at the rate at which they are sold to-day." Blankets of white wool, the color preferred by the Indians, were to go at the same rate. Guns that cost in New Orleans eleven livres were to go for ten large skins, and a three livre trade shirt would be exchanged for two large pelts. The Alabamas, in turn, offered not to deal with the English nor to allow them to settle in the Alabama country. While appearing to make the concession, Bienville asked that inferior limburg be sent to Louisiana! Also, the new plan would, of course, mean that more large and superior skins would reach the French commissary and fewer would reach the English — provided the arrangement was carried out.[20] The next year the governor ave the Choctaws the same privilege of trade at English prices — but this concession was in return for a Choctaw war against the Chicasaws who were defeating the French in some of the most vicious fighting in colonial history.[21]

As hard as the colonial officials and officers might try, they could not consistently match English quantity and price, and usually quality, over the years. The Alabama post, along with the others, was perenially short of goods desired by the natives. As an illustration, there were no white blankets for the Alabamas during the first year after the above agreement.[22] It could be, also, that the English in their turn gave the Creeks goods at cheaper prices than other Indians.[23] English settlers may have been inconsiderate to the Indians, but the traders in this area appear to have gotten along rather well after the Yamasee War. At the time Colonel Hastings became the chief factor in the Creek nation, 1718, the trade was a public monopoly.[24] Later, English traders were carefully licensed for a particular town or towns, and a genuine effort was made to curb abuses in trading with the Indians. There were, no doubt, many cases of mistreatment of Indians by the British, but the French records do not abound in instances of such in this area. In reading them, one would think the reverse was true.[25]

It is extremely difficult to estimate the amount of trade at the Alabama post. No doubt it varied tremendously, and certainly the French did not meet the full needs of the Indians in the area with any degree of consistency. Governor Daniel Coxe of Carolina was very concerned over the extent to which the French of Louisiana had cut into English commerce with the red men,[26] but the Louisiana trade did not begin to match that of the British in the Upper Creek country. Evidence as to the amount at the fort is contradictory. Two deserters from the Alabama garrison informed the Carolina authorities in 1723 that there was no commerce with the Indians there, that the Indians went to Okfuskee to trade with the English, and that the French exchanged ammunition for provisions.[27] However, what would appear to be a fairly reliable estimate based on a general census about the same time indicates that there were four or five small traders each of whom engaged in "commerce with the savages of his village" and took the commodities down to Mobile by *traversiers* or boats.[28] Also, as was pointed out earlier, officers and men engaged in trade. Mrs. Surrey in her *Commerce of Louisiana* (p. 348) estimates that the Alabamas supplied 3,000 skins in 1725.

This was about 6 per cent of the total she gives for the southern section of Louisiana — that is. Louisiana exclusive of the Illinois, Sioux, and Missouri Indians. This was three-fourths as many as produced by either the Chickasaws or Choctaws. The Abikas to the north were estimated as having furnished 8,000 and the Tallapoosas to the east, 5,000.

A memoir, apparently by Bienville in 1726, gave the identical figures as above except for the much more populous Choctaws whom he supplied 15,000 pelts.[29] No doubt the French at and about the Alabama post secured most of the pelts of the Alabamas and some others from the neighboring Abikhas and Tallapoosas, three of the most successful nimrods among the Indians in the southeast — when the French had commodities available for exchange. And there appears to have been at least gun powder and balls, even after years of blockade in the Seven Years or French and Indian War.

The inventory of stores in the *magazins* of the ten posts in Louisiana on January 1, 1731 totalled approximately 322,500 livres or the equivalent of perhaps 215,000 pounds of peltries. New Orleans storehouses had about two-thirds of the goods, and Mobile, Illinois, and Balize ranked in that order as other major depositories. Natchez was the fourth largest, having a slightly higher inventory than the Alabama post which was fifth. The latter held 4,000 livres of goods, perhaps worth 2700 pounds of pelts. Tombecbe was not far below the Alabama total value, but the Arkansas, Natchitoches, and Pointe Coupee-Tonicas were much lower in value.[30] Two years later, the total value was a little higher, but the increase was primarily in the New Orleans *magazin*. Fort Toulouse, like most of the others, had declined slightly, having 3,928 livres and 15 sous of commodities.[31]

It is true that the Louisiana officials gave special consideration to trade with the Alabama at times — when there was a special apprehension that they might go over to the English. It is true also that, as will be shown later, these Indians would get precious supplies even in times of extreme shortage. Even so, it is hard to believe that Tombecbe and Alabama each traded for as many as 50,000 skins annually as has been claimed. Colonel Robertson reported that he was given this figure by the officers in command of each post at the time of cession of the territory to the British.[32] The last governor of Louisiana, Kerlerec, claimed in a report in 1758 that the French were then furnishing only the same quantity of goods to the

Alabamas as when they came under French influence.[33] This amount
would have brought in only a few thousand pelts annually. The
official was continually begging the Versailles authorities to ship
additional commodities, so he probably was not too accurate in his
sweeping statement. The truth is probably between the two estimates.

The deerskins were of more value in England than in France
or Spain, so the British traders had the advantage of being able
to offer higher prices for pelts. They had also greater a quantity
of goods, a greater variety, and in some instances more attractive
styles and better quality. They had the lion's share of the Upper
Creek trade after Hastings succeeded in reestablishing it again in
1717. But despite the advantages they had, the traders from Albion
could not gain and hold the trade of the Alabamas. When the climax
of the contest for North America came, in the French and Indian War,
they had traders in all the other Creek towns of the area, but there
were no English traders in the half dozen Alabama villages in the
immediate vicinity of the fort.[34] This was approximately the same
number that the French traders monopolized in the first years of the
post.

The explanation for French success is partially, but only partially, due to the French determination to treat the Alabamas with
special care, to get goods to them even when in short supply. It is
true that commodities were of great importance in exerting influence
on the Indians. The Frenchmen who traded with the natives were
certainly practicing "dollar diplomacy". Commandant de Louboey
of New Orleans put it strongly when he reported in 1740 that commodities were "the main thing in all negotiations with the red man."[35]
But missionaries and officers were also diplomats working for French
hegemony in the Alabama country.

VII. *Fort Toulouse as a Missionary Center*

> ". . . in addition to the knowledge of God that they
> would impart to them, at least to some of them,
> nothing is more useful than a missionary to restrain
> the Indians, to learn all that is happening among
> them and to inform the commandants of the neigh-
> boring posts about it, to prevent the quarrels that
> may arise between the voyageurs and the Indians

and especially to see to it that the former do not sell
their goods at too high prices." Memoir on Louisiana, probably by Bienville in 1726.

"The French at the Allebawmaw . . . have had a Boat
come up lately deep loaded with a Priest, popery,
and Brandy. This Priest is come up, it seems, in
the Quality of Missionary for that Fort." William
McGillivray, to William Pinckney, Dec. 18, 1751.[1]

The French used their clergy both as missionaries and as diplomatic agents. This was the practice which had been followed in
Canada and Illinois and it had proved beneficial; hence an increased
use of them was proposed for Louisiana in the memoir quoted in
the above heading.[2] The Church authorities, the officials of the
Company of the West and the crown officials all favored the sending
of missionaries to Louisiana. The Bishop of Quebec had been given
authority over Louisiana, so Fort Toulouse was in the diocese of
far away Quebec. This was very awkward — but so was the government of Louisiana generally. The Carmelite order with a center
in Mobile was assigned the Alabama district for a time, but it was
placed, along with all of southern Louisiana, under the Capuchins
in 1722. The agreement was that the Capuchins of the French province of Champagne should place priests in the various posts. On its
part, the company would provide subsistence and maintenance or,
it was soon agreed, the clergymen had the option of taking 600 livres
instead. Also, there were to be expenses of half a year's payment
for the vestments for those who might be willing to travel to the
colony to serve. It was agreed that a missionary chaplain was needed
at the Alabamas.[3] and the Company offered to provide the following
for a priest at this as at other posts:

38 quarts of wine for use in the masses	42 francs
10 pounds of flour for bread for the same	3
30 pounds of wax candles	135
10 pounds of soap for laundering vestments	15
	195 francs

In addition, he was to be allowed 185 francs and 8 sous expenses
for a servant. These sums, for example, were in the budgets for
a priest at the Fort for 1724 and 1725.[4] The two budgets did not
carry the name of the priest, but one appears to have been there
by 1724. The Capuchin Superior reported to his Abbot in 1725 that

"the last missionary who was at the Alabamas was obliged to leave because for several months he had lacked wine for the mass" and had gone to the Apalachees where he still resided.[5]

The Superior painted a desolate picture of the clericals at the distant posts. He pointed to the very bad relations which commonly existed between the men of the cloth and the officers and claimed that a "little second lieutenant" was given precedence over the priests in drawing provisions; that these, always in short supply, would be distributed to officers first; that the latter would charge others exhorbitant prices for necessities; that wine, lights for the buildings, and subsistance for a servant were not supplied; and — he feared that Jesuits rather than Capuchins might be used to supply the unfilled positions at the posts.[6]

Jesuits were soon admitted to the missions at the posts, however, and the first member of the Society of Jesus to be sent to the Alabamas was Father Alexis (or Alexandre) Xavier de Guyenne. He was a native of Orleans who was in his early thirties when he was transferred from Canada for service in Louisiana. He was to spend thirty-six years in missionary work among the red men, to receive high praise for this service, and to remain with them until his death in the Illinois country in 1762. Father de Guyenne probably started work among the Alabamas in 1727 and remained for approximately three years.[7] In 1728 the budget showed that 800 francs were allotted to him for the year.[8] He must have had some success with the Alabamas, for he was chosen to attempt to found a new missionary post among the Cowetas, the Lower Creeks, "to keep the English away from them . . ."

This incident is an illustration of how the authorities hoped to use the Jesuits. Also it was probably the high point in missionary activity at the post. It was the Directors of the Company in Paris who took the initiative in this instance and marginalia on the correspondence demonstrates the interest and significance which they attached to it. They instructed Governor Perier and Ordonnateur de la Chaise to attempt the new mission; in turn, these men consulted the Vicar-General, Father de Beaubois as to the person to make the attempt. They agreed on Father de Guyenne, who was acquainted with the Creeks and understood English. At first, it was planned to have him make several journeys to the Cowetas and induce them to receive him, for "it would be imprudent to send a priest there before we were sure whether these Indians are willing to receive him and protect him from the insults of the English." In the meantime, another member of the first estate would be sent to the Alabamas, it was planned, and he would be instructed by the more experienced cleric. Then, the one who was best suited could be sent to head the new mission among the Cowetas.[9]

Later, it was decided that Father de Guyenne would "go to them in secular dress with an interpreter and a servant and that he should remain there three or four months in order to dispose them to receive him in another costume. He expects to succeed in it by means of some little presents." He left for the Chattahoochee area in late winter of 1729, having been allotted 1,000 livres or francs "to buy a suit and all the equipment necessary for such an enter-iprise," and the food for all three. As for the presents, he was to make a memorandum of them and present it for reimbursement.[10]

Despite the opposition of the English, he appeared to have been successful at first. He was able to have a cabin constructed in two villages. Then, however, his hopes collapsed; the cabins were destroyed by the Indians, although the English were blamed for the loss of them. He persevered for a time, then returned to the fort.[11] Shortly after this experience he left the Alabamas to continue his work in other parts of Louisiana.

Father Guillaume Francois Morand was the next Jesuit to be stationed there. But "the impossibility of exercising his Ministry, as regards both the Savages and the French, induced the Superior to recall him" from the mission.[12]

When the Company gave up Louisiana, the Crown resumed possession of the colony in 1732 and Bienville was again appointed governor. The instructions to him read that religion was still the principal object of the monarch, Louis XV, in establishing colonies. He was directed to encourage the missionaries and promote religion among Frenchmen and natives.[13] Jesuits were sent to the posts when they were available; perhaps one was available for the Alabama mission about half of the time. Jean B. Bossu, who was sent to the Fort in 1759 and who wrote a description of his visit, found that the position was vacant. The last priest, he explained, was Father Le Roi or Roy, who had been on bad terms with Captain Montberaut. This officer disliked Jesuits, and, according to one account, this particular one had opposed the sale of brandy to the natives.[14] According to Bossu, Father Le Roi had written the governor recommending that the officer in command be replaced by Captain Aubert, and Montberaut had intercepted the letter. Thereupon, Montberaut had asked the cleric if he had ever written anything against him, and the Jesuit had replied "strongly" that he had not. As a consequence, Bossu wrote, the officer showed the clergyman first the letter and then the door of the fort. The visitor closed his account laconically by saying there was "no longer a Jesuit Missionary to the Alabamas."[15] The last priest there was Father Predour. When the fort was evacuated in 1763, he returned to France.[16]

Crane concludes that French missionaries checked some of the worst abuses of Indians by the whites in French areas;[17] one cannot help but wonder, however, if there were missionaries at Fort Toulouse often enough to have much influence in that area.

Whereas the French made serious efforts at times to convert the natives, the British did not. When John Wesley arrived in Georgia in 1736, he considered the possibility of going into the Creek country in an effort to win them over to Christianity. Nothing came of this, however.[18] In the many-sided diplomacy — in the diplomatic efforts to win the friendship of the Indians — it was the French and their usual allies, the Spanish, who used their clergy.

VIII. *The Fort as a Diplomatic Center*

> "I never did see the French take any Think in Hand among those Creek Indians, but what comes to the same End as they intended it." William Sludder, trader in a nearby village of Oakechoys, to William Pinckney, South Carolina Indian Commissioner, Nov. 11, 1750.

It is a truism that diplomacy in the twentieth century includes a diversity of factors economic, psychological, demographical, and ideological as well as political. In the eighteenth century, Fort Toulouse had these qualities of a modern diplomatic post. Also, it was, in a sense, an armed, embassy. It was comparable in many respects to the collection of American forces and agencies in various friendly states abroad during the 1950's. Some of its military, economic, ideological, and demographical aspects have been reviewed.

Fort Toulouse also had its officers working more directly as agents in the conventional way foreign service personnel now work in embassies and consulates.

In addition to the trade, there were many types of economic aid to the Indians. Gifts were distributed among them regularly and on special occasions as reward for cooperation. Some of these were expected to enable the natives to develop trade, to raise the standard of living, and, of course, to buy more French goods as well. These were eighteenth century forms of what might later be called Point Four and technical aid.

La Tour was indignant that he had no gifts to distribute when he was sent to establish the fort. It was a thing which was unheard of, he complained. "La Tour does not have one sou's worth of merchandise" for gifts, Bienville indignantly wrote in September of 1717. The new governor was blamed by him for this unconventional practice, and he feared that the English, who of course had presents, might yet be successful.[1] The ordonnateur agreed with Bienville that the governor was perverse about sending presents to Indians; the chief executive was said to insist on ladling out the gifts himself, for the Indians did not come empty-handed. But what better occasion, for gifts, his critics asked, than this since "we have just been on the verge of losing" the Alabamas to the English.[2] It has been shown that the Toulouse officer met this emergency by requisitioning some goods for gifts from the Trefontaine brothers and scrounging around for others. It became the French custom to distribute a set amount of gifts to the principal Indians, although this was impossible to carry out during the frequent shortages of commodities. Major Diron in Mobile reported in 1728 that he distributed, for instance, fifteen to sixteen thousand livres or francs in merchandise annually.[3]

Merchandise to the Indians was given on special occasions also. One such instance in 1725 was unusual but direct. Bienville wanted peace between the Choctaws and the Chickasaws this time, so he encouraged the end of hostilities and a settlement by donating 5,000 livres of Limburg coats, powder, bullets, and other commodities.[4]

At the time the fort was constructed, and when the need for gifts there was reported to the Council of the Company, the typical gift of Governor l'Epinay, who was niggardly, was a gun, a coat, a blanket, ten pounds of powder, and the same amount of bullets, to a chief. His critics said that since a chief usually was accompanied by ten or a dozen other members of his tribe, the gifts were not sufficient.[5] Not long afterward, presents given to two chiefs of the Illinois and Kaskaskias consisted of: 4 trade guns, 2 blue and 2 red coats, 6 hats, 8 ells of limburg cloth, 96 *coutteaux passegrand* (probably large knives), 48 worm-screws for retrieving wads from gun barrels, 48 awls, 48 pieces of steel for striking fire from flint, 12 pounds of glass beads, 6 trade shirts, 4 pounds of vermillion, 20 small axes, 210 pounds of powder, 25 pounds of bullets and 4 plumes.[6] This was possibly more than normally given; at least it was more than given the same day to four Missouri country chiefs.[7] Large amounts were set aside for the purpose, however, and by 1732, 20,000 livres of commodities were budgeted and this was at the cost of the goods in France.[8] It was customary to make the gifts when the Indians visited the coast towns, though some were distributed at the Alabama post. Also, some tribes which were *persona non grata* in Mobile or New Orleans for a time or which feared attacks if they entered a rival's country on the way down, felt safe in going to that post. They could learn whether they might be received and might have a kind of safe conduct to the coast.

As a matter of fact, there were advantages in having the Alabama Indians considered to be neutrals, albeit benevolent neutrals, in the rivalry between the French and British. The fort was at times something of a sanctuary. In 1741 twenty-one of the leading men of the usually implacable enemies, the Chickasaws, went to the post to have commander d'Erneville intercede with Bienville to arrange peace between their nation and Indians to the north. As it happened, the Chickasaws made the visit at the same time that there was a session there between Choctaw and Abikhas chiefs. They had met "to put the seal on a treaty of peace" that Bienville had arranged between his allies, the Choctaws and the neutral Abikhas of the Upper Creek Nation. The Chickasaw spokesman used the occasion to express the hope that the Choctaws "will finally become weary of trading in our scalps" and to urge peace between the two nations.[9] The Alabama Indians and Lieutenant Hazeur of the Fort had had a part in arranging the Choctaw-Abikha peace. They had prevailed upon the latter to go to Mobile for a meeting with Bienville and the Choctaws. The interpreter at the fort, thirty or thirty-five Alabamas — chiefs with their wives and children — and half a dozen Tallapoosa chiefs had all gone down to Mobile to participate in the conference.[10]

The English noted with concern this kind of activity on the part of the French officers at Toulouse. In 1756, as the French and Indian War began officially, they noted with concern that chiefs of the Tellico people belonging to the Cherokees, their long-time allies, had gone for a conference at the fort. It was learned that, as they neared the fort, they saw leading Creek chiefs just leaving. The Tellicos stayed at Ochania during the visit, and Captain Montaut de Montberaut called them into a conference with their old enemies, the Choctaws. According to the report recorded by the English, the Choctaws expressed pleasure that the Tellicos had forgotten all past injuries and proposed that in the future there should be "one way of thinking" between them and both nations should look to the French for supplies; whereupon, Montberaut announced that the governor had promised to have good guns made to be given "to every man" in the Cherokee nation.[11] Although the French were in no position to carry out such a promise if it were made, the fort's officers had participated in conferences with three of the four "civilized nations" in a matter of days and were attempting to forge a front against the British of the Carolinas and Georgia.

The French relied primarily on the officers of the fort for their diplomatic agents; they performed as did resident ministers. The English, on the other hand, despatched officers, with small detachments. and other agents on special missions; one might say they performed as ministers on special missions. In either case, there was intense psychological warfare during war and peace. The English agents kept journals, sometimes in great detail, of their moves. Captain Tobias Fitch in the late summer and fall of 1725 visited the Tallapoosas and Abikhas, as well as the Lower Creeks. In the country of the first of these, almost in the shadow of the fort, he shamed the Indians for submitting to the will of the French officer in command. "I do not Endeavor to keep my Friends like slaves as the French do you," he declared. "But I am willing they 'should be like free men as they be and if the French can sell as Good Cloths as we do and as Cheap let them buy of the French." Then he taunted the officer in the "albaw-man Fort" about a negro slave who appears to have originally belonged to an Englishman, but had been bought by French subjects. Fitch had seized the slave to send him back to the English colonies. He told the Indians that if the French captain thought he had a better right to the slave, this officer should "Come and Take him Since he was Twenty men in the Fort and I have but Ten here." He then sent word to the

fort by the Indians that he had the slave and would await word
from the French for four days. The Alabama commander did send
back words rather than men, asking by what right or authority the
Englishman had seized the slave and declaring that if he had the
right, then he should refund the purchase price. Fitch's final taunt
was that his right was sufficient, but would be given only to his own
government; that, as for the purchase price, it was too great for
the government of Mobile to obtain![12]

General James Oglethorpe, governor of the new colony of
Georgia, travelled to the Lower Creek or Coweta country in 1739
and convoked an assembly of Indians, including the Abikhas and
Tallapoosas. He announced that he was on a diplomatic mission to
keep the French and Spaniards from fomenting an attack on the
English.[13] Lieutenant Hazuer, on the other hand, believed that the
presents by the British official and his diplomatic demarche were
unsuccessful in efforts to persuade the Indians to join in driving the
Spanish out of Florida.[14]

In the intense psychological rivalry, the Europeans resorted to
titles, special honors, and medals for their allies and supporters.
The French had a graduated scale for medal recipients. It was Mon-
goulacha, chief "a Medialle" of the Alabamons who led the large
Alabama delegation to Mobile in 1740 in serving as mediators between the Choctaws and the Abikhas. The white men also sought
to have their colors flown in the squares of the villages.[15] In this
manner their prestige at a given time might be determined.

Incidents of the psychological warfare are given by James Adair,
the Englishman who was best informed about the period and area.
A very literate person, he wrote *The History of the American Indians*,
published in London in 1775 after many years in the wildnerness.
He tells of various experiences with the French at what he frequently
referred to as the "dangerous Alebahma garrison". He found it to be
"directed by skillful officers" who inflamed the natives against his coun-
trymen and to be "supplied pretty well" with presents for them.[16] His
map of the Indian country has the word "Alebahma" in larger and
bolder type than "Mobile" or even "Charlestown". Adair tells of
having aroused the Indians to "shed a torrent" of French blood, although only in retaliation. As a consequence, when he made a visit
to the post in 1747, he was placed under arrest. So as not to give
umbrage to the natives, he was not imprisoned but was guarded by

two armed soldiers. He tells a dramatic story of an escape just an hour before he was to be sent down to Mobile in "the king's large boat." He relates with pride how he was able to make good his escape. He took to the briar patches of the bottomland, while the French hunted him by horseback on the paths, and Indians of the village only "150 yards" from the fort tried to follow his tracks.[17]

One can almost feel Adair's glee again as he relates another incident in the cold war. An unusually large caravan of English traders, a body of Choctaws, and (according to his history) 450 pack horses approached the post on the Lower Path from the east. Since the horses wore bells and the drivers shouted frequently, there was a great amount of noise generally on such trips; but on this occasion the British apparently decided to create the impression among their rivals that the dreaded attack on Fort Toulouse had come. He was sure that the approaching caravan created a terror among the members of the garrison at the fort that they would long remember.[18]

On occasion, Fort Toulouse was a refuge for disaffected British-ers. The French authorities were naturally suspicious of the emigres, and there appears to have been little effort to encourage them. John Canadet, an Englishman, and John Kennedy of Ireland were two men who fled to the fort in 1729, and were shipped first to New Orleans and then to France.[19]

One of the two most bizarre cases was that of Christian Priber, whom the British thought was on his way to the fort when he was finally seized and taken to Georgia. His danger was not in weapons, but in the manuscripts he was carrying: his plan for establishing a Utopia in the borderland between the French and British empires, and his dictionary of the Choctaw language. Like the later Saint Simonists, he wanted to set up among the Indians a model community based on the creed: "To each according to his needs, from each according to his capacity." The only private property an individual could hold in his proposed society would consist of a chest of books, paper, and ink. He had gone from Carolina to live with the Cherokees; after several years he had started in the direction of the fort when he was arrested by British officials as a subversive. He had worked for a peaceful Choctaw state which would have been independent of the British, but there is no reason to believe that he was an agent of the French as the English suspected. This "philosopher Utopian, linguist, scholar, friend of peace, of progress, of the Indian," who was a "solitary figure among the ruder folk who peopled the outer fringe of European civilization in America," was taken as a political prisoner to Georgia. He died there several years later. Truly, "he deserved a much better fate."[20]

In the year that hostilities of the French and Indian war began, there was a second bizarre case. A resident of "Charlestown" brought such a top-secret "cloak and dagger" story that it is difficult to determine his name, but it appears to have been Cambrede. He sought the ear of the commander of Fort Toulouse and was then sent down to the capital. His startling tale of intrigue was too much for the governor to handle, so Kerlerec reported the matter to the minister, and in code. The stranger had made a deposition that there were 800 families of the Catholic faith in his home city, that they were opposed to further British domination, and that they were encouraged by a report that a French fleet was to attack the fort guarding the city. He and three others had hatched a plot to aid the French conquest; they were prepared to put it into effect the moment the French vessels appeared. One of the conspirators was the "master cannoneer" of the twenty-one guns of the fort at the entrance to the harbor. The stranger had come to Louisiana to report this and to ask for a quantity of "cloux," or spikes. Apparently, these would be used in his plot to "spike" the guns and put them out of commission. He had not dared make these back in his own colony he explained, and had come to the French for them. The governor thought the project to be hazardous, and he must have been suspicious, for the English resident was first imprisoned. He decided this was a matter for his superiors and refused to do anything except by order of the minister. Consequently, the stranger with his story of intrigue was placed on the next ship to France,[21] and thus carried into oblivion as far as this writer knows.

Just as the fort was a goal for disaffected British subjects, it was a refuge for captive French nationals who might escape or be ransomed or rescued. Every so often Frenchmen who fell into unfriendly Indian hands would make their way or be sent to the post and then be able to return to French territory. As an illustration, two Chickasaw chiefs who wanted to get on the good side of the French ransomed two voyageurs who had been taken by the Natchez; afraid to go to the coast, the chiefs brought one of them to the fort in 1733.[22] Antoine Bonnefoy and some of his companions were seized by Cherokees on the Ohio and held them. He wrote a journal of his experiences in 1741-42, recounting his captivity, his pretended interest in Priber's republic (and nowhere in this does he even hint that Priber might have been a French agent), and his escape. He gives in detail the privations they suffered, the frustrations, the separation from his compatriots as they wandered in search of a route to Louisiana, and how he alone made his way down the Tallapoosa to friendly Alabama Indians who showed him the way to the fort. He arrived there the first of June, 1742, which he recorded as the "last day of my captivity." He was so emaciated and was in such poor condition that d'Erneville, once his superior officer, did not recognize him at first. Of course the Indians were given presents for their assistance.[23] These were only examples of the French nationals who returned via the post of the Alabamas. On other occasions, the garrison officers learned that kidnapped Frenchmen had been killed or made slaves and could not be returned.[24] Naturally, they and the emigres were "pumped" for information just as the British colonial officers grilled French deserters and Englishmen who made their way to the Carolinas and Georgia — and just as people from behind the Iron Curtain are now questioned by non-Communists.

The fort served as a listening post in these and many other matters. One of its important functions was to report fact and even rumor — just as embassies and consulates do today. The Indians were great gossips who enjoyed relating the activities of such English agents as Colonel Glover, for example, who made a trip to the area to win over the pro-French Choctaws, as well as Abikhas and others. Of course the commanding French officer also reported Spanish activity, but this was nothing like as frequent nor as significant to the French.[25]

There were many reports of the intentions and activities of hostile or potentially hostile Indians. Another very common subject of reports from the Alabama post was the aid which the British were giving to Indians who might be at war against the French. When he was in command, d'Erneville, for example, frequently passed on reports of the English aid given to the Chickasaws. In 1737 he wrote that the British were reported to have sent 200 men and 900 loaded horses; this was recognized as probable exaggeration, as it no doubt was.[26] Exaggerated and incorrect as it often was, this kind of military intelligence was of value in planning strategy.

Lieutenant Hazeur was able to report in the winter of 1738-39 that an English governor himself — apparently William Bull or Oglethorpe — was about to undertake a diplomatic mission and, thus warned, special efforts to meet and counteract this effort at rapprochement were taken.[27] When the French and Indians defeated Braddock and Washington near Fort Duquesne on July 9, 1755, the confirmation of it appears to have first been received in New Orleans via Fort Toulouse.[28] After Fort Tombecbe was established in 1735, the commanders at each post reported important information directly to each other. Some officers served at first one post and then the other, and this experience was no doubt helpful.[29]

In the section on the military history of the fort to the French and Indian War, it has been shown that, as far as is known, the troops were not used in hostile action against either the British or Indians; also it was rare that a direct threat of their employment was used as an instrument of policy. The one instance known to the author was in 1735. As indicated earlier, it was when two Englishmen, supported by several Tallapoosa chiefs, arrived in Akouitamopa to set up a trading post. This was an Alabama town only a league (less than three miles) from the fort. Lieutenant Benoist led eight men from his garrison and several Alabama chiefs to the village and "obliged" the British to withdraw.[30] Of course, there was always the potential use, the possibility that they might be employed; but the lack of hostile action emphasized the diplomatic rather than military nature of the post as far as its history is concerned.

The military contest between the rival British and French empires appears to have been almost inevitable and would come in the French and Indian or Seven Years War, 1756-63. When the hostilities began in the colonies before a declaration of war, how did the rivals compare in the Fort Toulouse sector of the frontier? How well had this military-diplomatic post succeeded in carrying out the objectives? Through the years, its prestige had varied, but generally, the English officials had expressed privately a healthy regard for the post. As deprecatingly as each contestant had spoken to the Indians about its rival, each regularly overestimated the power and the influence of the other. The British usually had a great advantage in quantity, quality, and price of commodities for sale. Also it has been estimated that South Carolina and Georgia had four times as many settlers as all Louisiana. But the Alabamas had never

been won over to the English, and as long as this was true, the
Creeks could not be counted on the side of the British. English
traders never were able to secure and keep the trade in the Alabama
villages. A French map drawn about 1756 gives the approximate
boundary of French influence as running several miles to the east
of the fort and in a north and south direction. It listed seven Alabama towns, with some 475 warriors, west of the line as under
French influence.[31]

British evidence as late as 1761 agreed that, although there
was an English trader in the great majority of Creek towns, they
had none in six Alabama villages which were credited with 265
hunters.[32] They were, essentially, the same Alabama villages which
the French won over to their side in 1717.

The Abikhas and Tallapoosas were occasionally pro-English, but
the Alabamas had been neutral or pro-French. Through the years,
the French officials assayed the sentiment of these key Indians;
time after time, the conclusion was satisfactory. Bienville reported
in 1741 that the Alabamas chiefs would be neutral if war came, and
that only a few Alabamas had agreed to join the English in a siege
of St. Augustine, despite a reduction in price of goods by one third.[33]
Bienville's successor reported three years later that they were loyal
despite plentiful English goods and a shortage of French.[34] During
the latter part of the War of Austrian Succession or King George's
War and when supplies were especially low and the Choctaws
were hostile, he could still report that the Alabamas were neutral
and the Abikhas and Tallapoosas were not anti-French.[35] This high
regard for the French existed in spite of the fact that the British
"would neglect almost nothing to achieve influence" among the
Alabamas.[36] "I have always had only a very good account to render
on the Alabamas who continue their good deportment," Governor
Vandreuil was still able to report four years later.[37] In turn, the
last governor of Louisiana, Kerlerec, could likewise report success
in 1756 in regard to their friendship.[38] In fact, the morale of the
garrison and the prestige and influence of the fort appears to have
grown in the late 40's and 50's as war approached.[39] With all the
economic advantages held by the British colonists, the French still
retained the goodwill of the Alabamas, and, usually, the Upper and
Lower Creeks were neutral. This was due to strategic position of
the French — and their diplomatic skill in its broadest sense.[40]

Fort Toulouse, as a French diplomatic post in the heart of the Creek Nation, had been successful in holding the frontier area which had been vastly extended when the post was constructed. In the fighting to come, would the British direct an expedition against Louisiana by land? Many factors would be considered in making the final decision, but one would be an estimate by them of the success of the military-diplomatic post at the Alabamas.[41]

IX. *The Show Down—The French and Indian War, 1754-1763*

> An "Expedition against the Albahma Fort by Land as hath been often talked of, would be powerfully opposed." Edmond Atkin to William Pitt, March 27, 1760, in reply to Pitt's proposal of such an attack. The king of France has abandoned Louisiana. (Governor Kerlerec to Minister Choiseul, Aug. 4, 1760.)

The period between King George's War, ending in 1748, and the French and Indian War, starting in 1755, was a truce rather than a genuine peace. In Europe, such protagonists as Frederick the Great on one side and Marie Theresa of Austria, Empress Elizabeth of Russia, and Madame Pompadour of France prepared for the war to come, known as the Seven Years War. Louisiana was given additional men and arms, though not a sufficient amount for the colonists to feel secure. The French government was much more occupied with the probability of war on the eastern border of France and preferred to concentrate their efforts on a war on the Continent rather than in distant colonies.

Governor Kerlerec, recognizing that Fort Toulouse was a "barrier between the English and us," had it rebuilt in 1751 under the direction of Engineer-in-Chief Brutin. The cost was 30,000 livres. This was almost half of Louisiana's annual budget for fortifications and military construction at the time, and was equal to the entire year's budget of 1755. Nevertheless, it was considered insufficient for a proper renovation. There was the usual rapid deterioration of the structures and they soon needed repairs.[1] But the British trader, Lachlan McGillivray, reported that it was "a pretty strong one" after it had been reconstructed.[2] The size of the garrison was increased somewhat, going up to about forty by 1754,[3] and increasing toward the end of hostilities to 48 or 49. The garrison consisted of a captain or lieutenant in command, 3 or 4 other commissioned officers who were lieutenants or ensigns of different ranks, a sergeant, as many as 4 corporals, a cadet or two, the tambour or drummer, and 37 or 38 fusiliers.[4] In reading the reports from Louisiana, this outpost seems to have been given more attention than most small forts, although the number of troops placed there was not relatively large.

On the eve of the declaration of war in Europe, the Minister of Marine notified Kerlerec that British attacks were expected to be directed against Canada and the islands rather than Louisiana; that, nevertheless, he should prepare the colony to repulse all attacks; and that if an attack should come, it would probably be on the coast.[5] He was correct in his prediction of British strategy. The Louisiana officers did not share this opinion, however, and if some of the Carolina officials had had their way, they would have attacked Louisiana. There were many anxious moments on both sides in the south. The French also decided that their principal military efforts in the colonies should be centered in the St. Lawrence and the Ohio basins rather than Louisiana.

As usual, the British concentrated their efforts on the sea and in the colonies. Such victories as that of Wolfe on the Plains of Abraham led to the surrender of Quebec in 1759, and, by the fall of 1760, the surrender of all Canada. There was an opportunity after that for the British to concentrate on Louisiana. One wonders why the attack never came, why such expeditions as the one against Havana were carried out — but not one against Louisiana. Perhaps the strength of the French among the southern Indians was a major explanation.

A surprising thing about the support that the French enjoyed among the Indians is that it was given in spite of a grave shortage of goods in Louisiana caused in part by British control of the seas. Also the home government did little to supply Louisiana with troops and materiel. Governor Kerlerec reported by 1758 that supplies and food were badly needed and this became a regular report.[6] It is interesting to note again how weak the rival governors would picture their own colony — yet how much each was feared by the other.

One of the first of many rumors one would expect during the war was picked up at Fort Toulouse in the summer of 1756. It was that the English had 500 men among the Cherokees where they were building six forts, and that two others were to be constructed among the neighboring Abikhas. The governor acknowledged that it was unverified, but he used it as a plea for more support from home. Of course, he played safe and increased the amount of scarce merchandise allotted to the trade at the Alabama post and urged the officer in command to redouble his efforts to hold the neighboring Abikhas and Tallapoosas in line.[7] Perhaps the increase in commodities did have the desired effect for it was now the turn of the Georgian officials to fear attack.

A friendly Indian, the Old Warrior of Tomotly, was sent by the British to gather information on the attitude of the Creeks; in January of 1757 he reported that the French had stepped up their trade and in his opinion the Creeks were under the influence of the French and lost to the British.[8] Whereupon, the Council and the House of Representatives of Georgia informed the governor of their fear of an attack from the west and cited as further corroboration a letter from South Carolina's governor. The legislature was apprehensive because the "greatest part of the Creek nation by the Influence of the French at the Alabama Fort are lost to us. . . ." The Creeks were believed to have made peace with the Choctaws and to have threatened the Chickasaws if they, too, did not join in an attack against the English. The chief executive of the Colony was asked to increase the company of "Rangers" to seventy men and to raise two new companies of the same size which would try to keep their Indian allies. Then as soon as able, the "Rangers" would go into the Creek country with friendly Indians and bring about the "Demolition of Albamah fort . . ." The governor agreed and the troops were raised,[9] although no campaign was undertaken.

Instead, the followers of the Union Jack put into motion an economic and political campaign which appeared to carry this flag to its greatest influence among the Creeks and even among the Alabamas, since the establishment of the fort. The British first stepped up their trade — or else the French could not fill the need for goods. The next summer, 1758, Governor Lyttleton of South Carolina could report that the "Creeks are not ill-disposed to us and we now carry on a very flourishing trade in their country but it is a fix'd principle with them to observe neutrality between us and the French that they may get supplies of goods and presents from both." He proposed an expedition against Louisiana's coast.[10] It is well known that

William Pitt the Elder himself proposed a series of offensive actions in this war. One proposal was an attack against Fort Toulouse rather than the coast. Governor Lyttleton supported the proposal although without retracting his own as an alternative. "As soon as ever I learn that you have determined to carry on Operations to the Southward I shall begin to take the necessary measures concerning the execution of His Majesty's Command relative to an Attempt on the Alabama Fort, and I hope when the matter is thoroughly examined it will not appear to be impractical," he reported. He enclosed evidence given by two experienced traders who claimed "an Enterprise against the Alabama Fort as likely to be attended with extreme difficulties," but he did not "give any great weight" to this testimony since it was to the interest of the traders to prevent the Creek Country from becoming a seat of war.[11]

While the military offensive was under consideration, preparations were being made for the Superintendent of Indian Affairs of the four southernmost colonies, Edmond Atkin, to work among the Creeks and then the Choctaws.[12] If successful, this mission would aid the military offensive; if no armed attack were made, it could discourage French offensives. By the time he reached the Creek lands, conditions were quite different, and he had a very difficult time at first. His report is a testimonial to the strong influence that Fort Toulouse exerted among the Alabama Indians in particular and the Creeks in general. When he set out, the Cowetas (Lower Creeks) and even the Cherokees had, he reported, openly exhibited English scalps. "The majority of the Indians in the area were in the interest of the French and the remaining dared not exert themselves for the English." Perhaps Atkin had the human weakness of exaggerating his own accomplishments, but he claimed that a pro-French confederacy had been planned. He reported that the Indians had agreed with the French to help capture Fort Loudoun, which had been built on the Tennessee River in 1757, and to eradicate the Chickasaws.[13] Nevertheless, since the French were unable to supply the wants of the Choctaws, their chiefs were willing to meet him in the Upper Creek country. Here, he was able to conclude a treaty with these natives on July 8, 1759, the first treaty, he reported with some pride, that the Choctaws as a nation had made with his state. He proposed that English guns and ammunition might be supplied to them along the coast. He reported also that although the Creek Nation was neutral, as usual, he had persuaded two leading chiefs to take English colors. Furthermore, they had agreed that when

English ships should appear at Mobile, they would head war parties against that port. Of course, Tombecbe and the Alabama fort would fall he added, if the rivers were closed.[14]

These results which he believed he had achieved did not come easily; and he had good reason to fear the strength of the fort. Its officers he wrote, almost succeeded in a plot to have him murdered and then all other Englishmen in the Nation liquidated. When he was speaking in Tookabachy square on September 28, 1759, one of the head warriors pretended to have gone berserk, and struck him six times with a pipe hatchet, he complained, adding that he later learned that the plot had been "concerted" at the fort and that his murderer was to have been a signal for falling upon all British-ers.[15]

Even before this attack, he had evidence of the loyalty of the Alabama to the French. He shows this in a legally phrased "Injunction by Edmond Atkin, Agent and Superintendent of Indian Affairs on the frontiers of Virginia, North and South Carolina, and Georgia to the British licensed traders in the Upper Creek country," bearing the date September 7, 1759. In it he forbade these traders to sell to the recalcitrant Alabamas. He called them the "stinking — Lingua Indians," living in the towns about the "French Fort" who "have never made or been included in any Treaty of Friendship made with His Majesty's subjects, but tho notoriously known to be entirely devoted to the Interest and Service of the French, . . ." They had been able to buy from British traders even in time of war with the French. Thus, he reasoned, these Indians who bought essential goods from the English, supplied the French garrison with "the common necessaries of life; so that the said Fort has been in fact supported for a series of Years by some of His Majesty's own subjects" despite the dangerous intrigues of its garrison. The French had tried to keep him out of the area by force, and even after arriving in the lower Creek lands had offered rewards for stopping him there. Some Alabama warriors had tried to do so at the hazard of their lives. He had already strictly enjoined these licensed traders near the Alabama towns from extending credit to them and to have no dealing with the two principal offenders, the towns of Tuskegee and Coosada. This had not produced the desired result, for "I have now been five weeks within 8 miles of the Albahma Fort, and those Indians have been advised to apply to me, and yet not one has come to give me his hand in the Indian manner, . . ." His mission had put the French to excessive expense in presents to the Creeks and in giving "almost incredible quantities of rum," and had exhausted their supplies. Suddenly, however, "fresh & large Presents were made by them without any Boats, arriving from Mobile;" these were cloth and blankets "got by the French from our Own Traders, . . ." Therefore, he forbade the traders under penalty of the utmost severity to give credit to, or sell to, or have any dealings whatever with any red men of any Alabama town or other persons knowing the goods to be for the Alabamas or the French.[16]

This was issued on September 7. Results must have seemed disappointing at first, for the attack on him came three weeks later. Nevertheless, there appears to have been compliance by the English traders, and the Alabamas became desperate or pretended that they were. It was on October 9 that Atkin's tactics at last appeared to be successful. On that date chiefs of the six towns asked to see him. When received they brought the usual tokens of friendship — clean white dressed deerskins which were placed "on his seat under him, and also others under his feet," — and acknowledged their distress. The French had been unable to supply them and the injunction had closed the English sources of supplies. The Indians of the six villages had conferred, "not one of them being at present away from home," and had empowered and authorized the chiefs to express "the General Voice of those Towns" and agree upon terms. Atkin readily drafted a "Treaty of Friendship & Commerce." This was not an alliance; but it was the first such treaty with the Alabamas, at least since the fort was constructed in their midst.

It was signed the next day at Tookabatchie by the Superintendent for His Britannic Majesty as party of the first part and marks were made by chiefs of Coosada, Tuskegee, Ockchoy, Little Ockchoy, and Weetunky, on the same date. Opoyheatly, Proprietor of the Ground & Mico of Puckana, did not make his mark until a week later. One wonders how much soul searching must have been done during the week by the chief of this village so close to the post.

The treaty contained an acknowledgement that since the fort was built[17] these natives had "had the most intimate connection with the French, & been particularly serviceable to them many ways more than other Indians;" yet at the same time, most of their clothing and other supplies had been obtained from British traders. The Indians acknowledged also their need for goods and, in return for renewal of trade with the English at the same rates as other Creeks, they promised to "live in perfect Peace" and friendship with them.

Various conditions were attached. The Alabamas were to buy for their needs only and not buy or sell any goods for use by the French. They could buy from only two traders either at the Mocolussah village on the Tallapoosa or Little Tallassee on the Coosa. The Indians were enjoined from obstructing trade or molesting traders passing along the Lower Path to the Choctaw Nation. They promised not to "carry or send the French Talks about to other Indians," nor act as couriers to Mobile or Tombecbe. In fact, "they shall not take part with the French in any thing whatever, against or to the prejudice of his Britannick Majesty, or any of his subjects." Furthermore, they were to give satisfaction for any injury to persons or effects of George II's subjects. As a sign of the declaration of friendship, the Alabamas were to set up "the Suit of English Colours" in each town's square within two days and display the said colors on all public occasions and whenever a talk relating to the English was held.[18]

The treaty was sealed by the exchange of gifts. The Alabamas had at last agreed to a formal treaty of friendship and commerce with the English and to end their trade with the French. One wonders what emotions were experienced by the signers. Surely Atkin must have congratulated himself on his apparent success with the elusive Alabamas. But if the English agent had any illusions about the sweeping agreements the Alabamas had made, they did not last long. One month to a day, the French were able to have a fifty-horse caravan bound for the Choctaws interrupted. The horses were recovered and in another month the pack train went through.

When Atkin returned to Charleston in March of 1760, his first hurried report to William Pitt did not mention the Alabama treaty, but he was quite optimistic about English prospects. He believed an invasion of Louisiana could succeed. "The Chickasaws, the Creeks [he always referred to the Creeks as being separate from the "Alabama Nation"] the Choctaws are able and probably will give powerful assistance," he concluded. "But an Expedition against the Albahma Fort by Land as hath been often talked of, would be powerfully opposed."[19] Since it was understood that the Cherokees were friendly, his compatriots had all four of the "Civilized Tribes" on the English side except the Alabama segment of the Creeks — provided, of course, his estimate was correct. He actually seemed to feel, as optimistic as he was, that Mobile and even New Orleans might be easier to capture than Fort Toulouse, with its strategic position on the distant frontier and its Indian allies.

His estimate was given six months after Quebec had fallen and only six additional months would pass before Montreal and all Canada would be surrendered to the British. When Canada fell to the English, would it not seem logical to conquer the remaining French colony, Louisiana, with its Mississippi Valley and Gulf area, and thus dominate all of the eastern half of North America? But an attack against Louisiana was not attempted. Perhaps the War Office and Admiralty records will indicate the variety of reasons why the attack was not made. It is likely, however, that one reason was the antagonism and hostility displayed by the very Indians Atkin had thought he had won over to his side. In his negotiations in Tukabatchee, it should have been obvious to him that it was the Choctaws who were determined to reach an agreement with the English. The Upper and Lower Creeks were not enthusiastic. As a consequence, they soon fell upon the English traders and killed a dozen of them. Governor Kerlerec credited this to the "contingent des Alibamous," meaning the Abikhas, the Tallapoosas, the Alabamas, and the Cowetas. They were also urging the Cherokees to seek an alliance with the French and to make war on the British.

This was wonderful news to the French capital, but it raised a serious problem. The English were not ones to accept defeat readily. They would seek a renewal of the Choctaw trade, but they would not trust the Creeks until these had shown some overt sign of their friendship. This could only be an act against the French. Such an act might be against Fort Toulouse. "The Poste des Alibamous, as is well-known, is one of the principal keys of His Majesty's domains on this continent," he reasoned, so it was necessary to assure the Indians of French support and not to ignore their needs. But the difficulty was the shortage of commodities. To solve the problem, Governor Kerlerec called an Extraordinary Council of War. Here it was voted unanimously to dig into the dwindling supplies of the colony in order to send goods to "the Alabama contingent" and also the Cherokees.[20]

French success continued. The Choctaws were won over and

agreed to attack the Chickasaws.[21] More significant still, the Creeks and the Cherokees opened a major campaign against the English colonists.[22] The relatively new frontier fort of Loudoun was captured and Fort Prince George and other English establishments were threatened. Lieutenant Governor William Bull, while acting-governor of South Carolina again suggested that the most effective way of managing the Indians was to reduce or take Mobile and New Orleans. He requested that 2,000 troops be supplied for the protection of the western frontier.[23] Bull acknowledged that the "Albama Fort" had had a hand in influencing the Indians, but he did not suggest an attack against it. The Louisiana governor must have agreed with his counterpart that the post's officers should have credit, for Major Develle at Mobile and Lieutenant La Noue in command at the fort were both given bonuses in 1760, and these were quite rare in this period.[24]

Despite this unique opportunity to recoup some of its losses in Canada, the home government did practically nothing to aid Louisiana. Governor Kerlerec complained that the king had "abandoned" Louisiana.[25] In the extremity in which he found himself, other councils of war were held in New Orleans and in Mobile. One stands out above the others, an extraordinary council of war in the capital in February, 1761. The governor explained to the members that the government warehouses in New Orleans were down to three days supply of rice and corn. There was a serious shortage of food also at Mobile, Tombecbe, and the Alabama garrisons. Furthermore, the last harvest of the Choctaw and Creek tribes was a total failure, and they were in dire distress. It was indispensable, he continued, that the garrisons, inhabitants, and Indians about these posts be supplied. The law provided that only the *ordonnateur* had the authority to purchase provisions, but Rochemore had stubbornly refused to do so. The failure to send provisions to the Creeks and Choctaws "could affect the colonies as much as European enemies," the governor added. He proposed that Rochemore be given eight days to procure enough provisions to enable Mobile, Tombecbe, and Toulouse "to hold the Indian nations" and maintain themselves in a state of defense. If the *ordonnateur* refused, then the other officers should buy provisions anyway. He asked for a written opinion from each member. Not one member stood with Rochemore. While some were not ready to go over his head, a good majority supported the governor.[26] These extreme measures explain how the stocks in the Alabama *magazin* held up as well as they did.

The English, however, sent troops to the southern frontier. A large contingent was sent to South Carolina in 1760, and the next year a larger number of Highlanders and Colonial soldiers were dispatched. These forced peace upon the Cherokees and stabilized the frontier,[27] but thy were not directed against the Creeks.

Intrepid British traders then returned to the Creek territory; but when James Montgomery came from there in June, 1762, he brought disturbing reports once again. These confirmed the news that troops had been landed at New Orleans, as had two shiploads of goods, the only ones from "Old France" in five years. A boat load of presents for the Creeks was on the way to the Alabama fort, it was reported to Governor Thomas Boone of South Carolina, who added, "Am apprehensive, this bodes no good to the English."[28]

The fighting on the mainland of North America was over, however. Spain entered the war early in 1762 and England's offensive was directed against Havana in July.

Although it had been badly neglected, France's officials had not actually abandoned Louisiana during the hostilities. Some of them did believe that it could not be held after losing Canada, but others suggested moving the French Canadians to Louisiana. As the war dragged to its close, French diplomats began to give thought to the boundaries of Louisiana over which they could expect the usual haggling during peace negotiations. When the discussion of terms got underway, Louisiana was still in the possession of the French. There seemed little likelihood that the colony would pass from French hands.[29]

X. *The Fort in the Treaty Negotiations*

> The boundary of Louisiana on the east should run from the mouth of the Perdido River to Fort Toulouse, from there to the westernmost point of Lake Erie, etc. (French Memoir of Aug. 10, 1761)

Attention to the future boundaries of Louisiana was given by French officials as early as 1761. If Canada were ceded to Britain, it was expected that Louisiana would be retained. "The principle which should mark the boundaries between Louisiana and Canada ought to be that, where the Governor of Louisiana sends garrisons, he has charge of the government of that area."[1] In such a case, Fort Toulouse would become a "chief point for garrisons." One proposal was that it be made one of six large garrisons: Mobile, Tombecbe, Toulouse, Massaic, Joncaire, Dequesne, Ste. Anne des Ouyatanons. As is the way with diplomats and other bargainers, the French put forward more extensive claims than they expected to get, proposing that France have even the land of the Cherokees. Pitt countered with the idea that there should be a large neutral area between the Ohio and the Appalachacola.[2]

Soon however, Versailles diplomats proposed that the boundary of Louisiana run from the Gulf of Mexico at the mouth of the Perdido River, then to Fort Toulouse, thence to the westernmost point of Lake Erie, on to the eastern point of Lake Huron, and from there to Lake Abitibi.[3] Naturally, William Pitt rejected the northern portion of the proposed boundary "as inadmissible", since it had been considered as a portion of Canada, and it had been agreed that Canada should go to the British. As for the Creek, Chickasaw, and Choctaw lands, the English diplomats claimed that these had always been under the protection of their government, and should remain so.[4]

While some of the advisers at the court still urged that extensive aid be rushed to Louisiana, others recommended that France might as well cut its losses and give it up completely. The colony had been a drain on French resources and French policy had been directed more toward continental expansion and interest than colonial. As a consequence, France now offered to cede New Orleans and all Louisiana west of the Mississippi to its ally, Spain, and the remainder to its enemy, Britain.[5] Just before Christmas of 1762 Minister Choiseul could express his happiness that Louisiana would soon be taken over by Spain which would hereafter bear the expense of maintenance.[6]

The news that the mother country was now truly and openly deserting Louisiana was received with consternation by the colonials. Governor Kerlerec received the preliminary terms of the treaty of peace with the greatest concern on two counts: The effect the terms would have upon his Indian allies and what the infuriated Indians might do to the French colonists. It was true, he wrote the minister, that France would be free of its enemies; "but it is not the same, my lord, with the great number of nations which are in our area which have sacrificed their life and their tranquility in order to serve the French." He was particularly concerned with the reaction of the Cherokees and the Alabamas (a term he used to indicate all the Creeks). When they should learn that their lands had been ceded to the English, he predicted trouble from them. He expected them to say haughtily that the French had no right to cede Indian lands, that the red men were not yet all dead, and that they would know what to do! Furthermore, he added, these comments would be made with menaces which would throw consternation among all the inhabitants and garrisons exposed to incursions by the Indians. He predicted "many difficulties," even violence, in evacuating two posts, those of "Tombecbe et les Alabamoux."[7]

The garrison numbered forty-eight officers and men.[8] A census which the governor had forwarded to France in 1758 indicated that there were 160-odd French civilians living in the vicinity of Fort Toulouse.[9] The great majority of emigrants from France would no doubt wish to move out of the new English colony, but that would take time.

In his fear for the life and property of the French, the Governor determined to take an extreme measure of precaution. He planned to invite twenty-five or thirty notable Choctaws and as many Creeks to New Orleans on the pretext of a conference with them. Once there, he would hold them as hostages. He would treat them with kindness, as always, but he would inform them that they should dispatch four men to each nation to notify their fellow tribesmen that the governor was holding them as hostages for the security of the garrisons and the inhabitants until they could be withdrawn. He feared that even the capital itself might be raided by the Choctaws.[10]

This was a bizarre plan, and there would be many difficulties connected with the evacuation of the Fort Toulouse; but such extreme measures would not, in the end, prove to be necessary.

XI. *The French Evacuation in 1763 and the British Decision Not to Garrison the Fort*

> "The English give me more trouble here, Monsieur, than the savages, . . ." (Director-General d'Abbadie to Governor Kerlerec, Mobile, Nov. 6, 1763.)
>
> "The path to Mobile was once clear, but is now grown up, . . ." (An Alabama chief as quoted in a John Stuart letter of Dec. 2, 1770, British Transcripts, LC, PRO, C. O. 5, 72:227.

The officer who was assigned to oversee the evacuation and transfer of the territory to the British was Director-General d'Abbadie. He was instructed to act as promptly as possible,[1] but it was an extremely frustrating assignment for this officer. The governor continued to anticipate serious difficulties in evacuating forts Toulouse and Tombecbe and predicted delays as a consequence.[2] There was, certainly, cause for genuine concern over possible Indian recriminations, and there were many delays; but d'Abbadie found himself more vexed by the British than threatened by the Indians. The delays were due in large part to difficulties he had with the English over the interpretations of the terms of the treaty concerning whether ordnance and various military stores were to be surrendered. The British, too feared Indian hostility. They blamed the French for stirring up the Indians against the victors and called on the French to protect them against Indian incursions. Mobile was formally evacuated on October 20, but greater difficulty was encountered in the transfer of Tombecbe and Toulouse. The English insisted on acquiring the artillery and munitions still in the latter posts, and "objections are born every instant," d'Abbadie exclaimed. He finally agreed to leave the ordnance and military stores which were at the two inland posts. He informed the British Commandant in Mobile that he agreed to this because of his concern for the safety and security of the new occupants.[3] But he gave his superior another reason: "Between you and me," he explained, "it is because it is impossible to remove the artillery." The British garrison destined to take over Tombecbe was readied to leave Mobile on November 6 for the twelve or thirteen day trip upstream. As expected, greater difficulty was encountered in the evacuation of the Alabama post. The British officer insisted on a guarantee against Indian incursions there, even after the agreement to leave the French munitions. The French director-general was no more inclined to give the guarantee than he was able to carry it out. Running desperately short of food and supplies there, d'Abbadie pressed Colonel Robertson to send his new garrison to the fort. When the French officer indicated that he would have the Alabama post evacuated anyway, the English commandant announced that if the garrison were brought down to Mobile before the new English garrison arrived, France's troops would be held as prisoners of war! Nevertheless, the decision reached by the director-general was first, to summons all but twenty men and one officer to Mobile; then to have the Alabama chiefs come to Mobile where they could be addressed in the presence of the suspicious British; next, he would immediately order the remaining twenty-one members of the garrison to descend the river to Mobile. The officers of George III could do what they judged proper, for "I had rather see this garrison prisoner of war in Mobile than allow it to die of famine in a post where I am not able to support it." "What an assignment," the exasperated officer exclaimed in a report to the governor, "to have to deal with men drunk with their success, and who regard themselves as masters of the world!"[4]

The cocky British had their problems also. They had been debating among themselves whether to demolish the two posts or garrison them. As early as May, 1763, Jeffrey Amherst doubted the wisdom of their demolition and that of Fort Loudoun. His opinion was that "Indians will always be best Neighbors when they see that We are in a state to Defend Ourselves . . ." However, the matter was left up to the local authorities who were the best judges of the Indian "humor".[5]

The Alabamas made it clear that they wanted only British traders, not a garrison. Two of their chiefs, Tamatle and Toupalga, as spelled in the French reports, came down with the inhabitants in the Toulouse area when they descended the river. Others came down at the request of d'Abbadie (and to receive presents), and they did not hide the fact that they were "enraged" to see the English occupy their lands.[6]

The final British decision was to send no garrison to the Alabama fort. It was reached by Colonel Robertson, who, if he did not use good grammar, did use sound logic when he explained:

> I have made it a rule, to take no post, but such as could be reliev'd or reinforced however ill the Indians may be disposed.

> And consider'd a small garrison out of reach of
> succor, where the Indians can prevent Supplys, as
> so many hostages in their hands.
> It was for this reason that I decline sending from
> Mobile a garrison to Albama, having found the
> Creek averse to receive one.

If he had then been in command, he explained, he would not have
sent even the small detachment to Fort Tombecbe.[7]

Thus it was that the British did not send a garrison to the
Alabama post. Sometime during the winter of 1763-64, the last
French garrison under the command of La Noue or Lanouie[8] evacuated the fort after more than forty-six years of occupation. Certainly, it was after the middle of November, 1763[9] and before
January 15, 1764. Furthermore, it was finally accomplished "without
the least accident."[10]

When the cannon were spiked, the excess powder dumped into
the Coosa, and the *fleur de lis* lowered for the last time, the French
phase of the history of the site came to a close. The establishment
of Fort Toulouse had pushed the boundaries of Louisiana far into
what had been, before the Yamasee War, an area under English
domination. The small detachment carried out its assignment remarkably well. When the French lost Louisiana, the defeats came
on other frontiers, not at the Alabama post. When post-war boundaries were discussed, the French had the best basis — occupation — for
claiming the area with the fort as the boundary. It had held the
area despite determined British efforts to win over the Alabamas
and turn all Creeks against the Louisianians. No other French post
was in such close proximity to the rivals, in such an exposed position
as Fort Toulouse. None was under such continual pressure from
the British.

At all times, the most skillful diplomacy was essential. The
French had to resort on occasion to extraordinary efforts to hold
their advanced post: Cheaper prices for their goods at the Alabama
post, the manufacturing of goods designed for the particular taste
of the Indians in that area, higher pay for the members of that
garrison, councils of war to secure goods to be rushed to the post.
Not once did the French lose the benevolent neutrality of the Alabamas, and at times they had the whole Creek Nation as allies.
In fact, one wonders whether there have been many times in history

when there was such a good relationship for so long a period between the soldiers of one race stationed in another's land, especially in the face of continual efforts to lure the inhabitants to another cause.

XII. *Sequel*

"No other military post within the limits of the State of Alabama has a background equal in importance to that of Fort Jackson, . . . [where] Gen. Andrew Jackson made peace with the Creek Nation, after one of the most bloody Indian Wars in the history of our country." Lieutenant Colonel Howard L. Landers, U. S. House Reports, 71st Cong., 2nd. Session, III, 17-18.

The failure of the British to occupy[1] the fort did not bring to a close the historic importance of the site. There was to be still another exceptionally significant period for it during the national history of the United States. There were to be some decided contrasts and striking similarities to the French era when the Americans rebuilt the fort.

The site became the property of the latter by the Treaty of Paris in 1783. During the War of 1812, many of the Creek Indians were prepared to support the British rather than the new American state. When whites on the frontier were attacked, General Andrew Jackson carried out a most successful campaign against them. As he advanced, he established a line of posts from Tennessee into South Alabama. His outstanding victory was at Horseshoe Bend up the Tallapoosa River from the site of the fort. This was on March 27, 1814, and shortly afterwards he directed his troops to the junction of the two rivers. Jackson and his Tennessee army reached there on April 17 and began the construction of a new fort, making use of the old moat, about all of value which remained. The general insisted on a strong and well-manned post. It was planned as the point at which the chain of forts from Tennessee would be joined by another starting from Georgia. But such Indian chiefs as William Weatherford who made their way to the new station came to make their peace with the Americans, not to attack.

Major General Thomas Pinckney arrived on April 20 and assumed command. This General, who outranked Jackson, promptly named the new post Fort Jackson in honor of the victorious general who had started the reconstruction of the fort. From that time, many people have known the site as Fort Jackson.

Pinckney remained there while Jackson returned to Tennessee. This was only a temporary absence, however. Jackson was soon made a major general and was back at the post by July 10. He had the reconstruction of the fort completed and turned his attention to Spanish and British intrigues as well as a peace treaty with the Creeks. The chiefs of the latter met the two American commissioners, Jackson and Colonel Benjamin Hawkins at the post. Long discussions followed when the Indians learned with dismay the extent of the American demands. It was here that the Treaty of Fort Jackson was signed on August 9, 1814. This meant that at least half of all the land of the Creek nation was surrendered. Furthermore, the land taken by the whites would separate the Creeks from the Spanish to the south, the Choctaws to the southwest and west, and the Chickasaws to the west and northwest. Thus, the Creeks would be in no position in the future to be a threat to the United States. It meant also that Jackson could leave a smaller garrison at the new fort and could take the remaining troops to the Gulf with some confidence that the line of communication would be safe. He was to go on to Mobile and New Orleans — and to greater fame as the victor in the Battle of New Orleans.

The new fort, unlike the original, was intended as a fort against the Indians. Like Fort Toulouse, there were no hostilities there, however. Both were used as significant centers for negotiation with the natives.

There was a tragic similarity in another respect. During the American occupation there was a serious mutiny. Although comparable in some ways to the one in 1721, it is doubtful if any of the raw recruits who mutinied had ever heard of the earlier one and its boody outcome. The climax came on September 20, 1814, when some one hundred men, claiming that their terms of enlistment had expired, defied their officers and marched back to Tennessee. Whereas the French mutineers had tied up their officers, eaten a hearty meal, lighted their fuses, and marched off with drums beating, the Americans defied their officers, slaughtered cattle in the public pens, cooked their rations for the trip, and marched away shouting and firing their guns. This act seriously weakened the post and the line of communications, something which Jackson could not take in good spirit. Over two hundred men in all were taken into custody and tried in Mobile. Six were executed on February 21, 1815.

The Fort was stocked with a large supply of provisions and a garrison was maintained there until 1817.[2]

By this date, settlers were coming into the area, and it is not surprising that the site was chosen for a town. One was laid out just above the fort; naturally, it was named Jackson. When Montgomery county was first formed, the county court was held there. For various reasons, however, it never did attract many settlers. They preferred to settle in Montgomery to the south or Wetumpka to the north.

As time passed, the number of residents in the peninsula formed by the two rivers has declined. As this account is written, the area is primarily in pasture land. There is only an occasional farm house in the vicinity. Visitors to the site find little to remind them of its history. It is marked by a granite shaft placed by the Society of Colonial Dames in 1912. The state of Alabama has purchased several acres of land on the river bank as a start toward preservation of the site. There is now a Fort Toulouse Memorial Park Association which is attempting to have the area made a national historic site and placed under the jurisdiction of the National Park Service. It is hoped that in this way the site can be properly marked and preserved for posterity.

NOTES

1. THE POTENTIALITIES OF A FORT AT THE HEAD OF THE ALABAMA RIVER

[1]*The Southern Frontier, 1670-1732* (Durham, N. C., 1928 and Ann Arbor, Mich., 1956), p. 255 or 256. This is a superior review of the rivalry for the area. It uses many manuscript colonial records, particularly British.

[2]"The Alabama-Tombigbee Basin in International Relations, 1701-1763" (Unpublished Ph. D. Dissertation, University of California, 1928), p. ii. This is a 324 page account of the contest for the area. The author used the best sources, both public and private, which were in print at the time. It is unfortunate that this superior study was not published.

[3]The high water of 1886 caused the Tallapoosa to cut a new channel and meet the Coosa less than a mile below the site.

[4]Mark van Doren, ed., *The Travels of William Bartram*, (New York, 1928), p. 355.

[5]See the section on economic activities (V) and Crane, *Southern Frontier*, p. 326, and *Passim*.

[6]*The History of the American Indians* (London, 1775), 6. 258-60. Crane reaches the same conclusion on p. 185 of his *Southern Frontier*.

[7]Grace King, *Jean Baptiste Le Moyne, Sieur de Bienville* (New York, 1893), pp. 131-36; Reynolds, *"Alabama-Tombigbee Basin"*, pp. 39-74, *passim*; Hamilton, *Colonial Mobile*, p. 73.

[8]Bienville to Pontchartrain, Mch. 2, 1712, Dunbar Rowland and Albert G. Sanders, eds., *Mississippi Provincial Archives, French Dominion* (Jackson, Miss.), III, 172. These three volumes of documents are instructions sent to colonial officials and reports by these officials which have been copied from the French archives, translated, and edited. They are classified as Archives du Ministere des Colonies, Serie A C 13 and Serie B, Correspondence generale Louisiane. They constitute a major printed source for the history of Fort Toulouse.

[9]Bienville to Pontchartrain, June 15, 1715, *ibid.*, III, 183.

II. CONDITIONS AND EVENTS LEADING TO THE ESTABLISHMENT OF THE FORT

[1]Justin Winsor, *The Mississippi Basin, the Struggle in America between England and France, 1697-1763* (Boston, 1895), pp. 85-86.

[2]Bienville to Ponchartrain, Jan. 2, 1716. *Miss. Prov. Arch., Fr. Dom.*, III, 195-96. Bienville was so outraged at the governor's treatment that in one paragraph of an official report he first charged that Cadillac treated him as if he were a "Corporal" and a few sentences later as if he were a "sergeant." (Bienville

to Raudot to the Council Jan. 20, 1716, *ibid.*, 199). It was John Law, whose claims (that the province abounded in precious metals) were declared false by Cadillac, who brought about the imprisonment (Clorence W. Alvord, *The Illinois Country, 1673-1818* (Springfield, Ill., 1920), p. 151.

³ King, *Bienville*, p. 148.

⁴See his later comments in a memoir, probably in 1726, *Miss. Prov. Arch., Fr. Dom.*, III, 512 and Bienville to Maurepas, April 30, 1735, *ibid.*, I, 263.

⁵Bienville to Pontchartrain, June 15, 1715, *Miss. Prov. Arch., Fr. Dom.*, III, 183. He was also able to get the ordonnateur or commissary general to approve expenditures for presents to various Indian tribes which he had refused Cadillac. (See a relatively new study by Marcel Giraud, *Histoire do la Louisiane francaise*, Vol. I, *Le Regne de Louis XIV*, (1698-1715) Paris, 1953, pp. 300-02. This volume deals at some length with the contest between the British and French for control over the Indians. A second volume of this superior work based heavily on the best French and English sources, has the sub-title *Annees de Transition*, (1715-17), was published in 1958. Agents were despatched and were successful. (*Ibid.*, II, 303.)

Professor Giraud read the manuscript of this history of Fort Toulouse and and pointed out various errors which it contained. The author is grateful to him for his criticisms which were received in time to be incorporated in the first half of the study.

⁶Crane, *Southern Frontier*, p. 168. ⁷*Ibid.*, 162.

⁸Bienville to Pontchartrain, Sept. 1, 1715, *Miss. Prov. Arch., Fr. Dom.*, III, 188. Andre Penicaut in his *Annals of Louisiana from 1698-1732*, translated by Richebourg McWilliams (Baton Rouge, 1953) p. 165 says the principal chief of the Alabamas proposed the latter part of 1715 that the French construct a fort among them at the expense of the Indians.

⁹Crane, *Southern Frontier*, p. 133. ¹⁰*Ibid.*, 97.

¹¹Bienville to Pontchartrain, Sept. 1, 1715, *Miss. Prov. Arch., Fr. Dom.*, III, 188. The Alabamas were not numerous. A British report of this date gave them only four towns and 226 fighting men, whereas the Tallapoosa up the river of that name and the Coosas (or Abikhas) living above on the river of the same name were each over twice as numerous. (Crane, *Southern Frontier*, pp. 134-map following p. 326 of the 1928 publication.)

¹²*Ibid.*, 255-56.

¹³Giraud, *Historie de la Louisiane*, I, 304; Crane, *Southern Frontier*, p. 256. It looked for a time in the autumn of 1715 as if Cadillac would agree. (Bienville to Pontchartrain, Sept. 1, 1715, *Miss. Prov. Arch., Fr. Dom.*, III, 185.)

¹⁴Cadillac to Pontchartrain, Jan. 2, 1716, Pierre Heinrich, *La Louisiane sous la Companie des Indes, 1717-1731* (Paris, n.d.) p. lxxiv.

¹⁵Bienville to Pontchartarin, Jan. 2, 1716, *Miss Prov. Arch., Fr. Dom.*, III, 192-93. See also Duclos to Pontchartrain, June 7, 1716, *ibid.*, 204.

¹⁶Duclos to Pontchartrain, June 7, 1716, *ibid.*, 204-05.

¹⁷W. L. McDowell, (ed.) *Journals of the Commissioners of the Indian Trade.* September 20, 1710-August 29, 1718 of the *Colonial Records of South Carolina* (Columbia, 1955), pp. ix, 325.

¹⁸*Ibid.*, 169. ¹⁹*Ibid.*, 188-89. ²⁰ Crane, *Southern Frontier,* 257.

²¹The Council of Marine, to Cadillac and Duclos, Paris, Feb. 15, 1716, French Transcripts, Library of Congress. Archives du Ministere des Colonies, Serie B, Vol. 38, folio 287-88 *verso.* Louis XIV's memoir of Dec. 27, 1714 on the same matter was copied and sent with the original. These are selections from the original colonial manuscript records of France which have been transcribed and are now in the U. S. Library of Congress. They were loaned to the author for this study. Hereafter a citation such as the one above will be "French Transcripts, LC, AC, B 38: 287-88 vo. See also, Crozat to the Council, date missing, ibid; C 13c 1:293-94 vo. These deposits and the ones described below constitute the most significant collections of manuscript materials on the fort's history. See also Minutes of the Marine Council held at Le Louvre, Paris, Sept. 8, 1716, French Transcripts, Mississippi Department of Archives and History, Jackson, Miss., Archives du Ministere des Colonies, Serie C 13, Vol. 4, folio 323-24. These are still other French colonial manuscript records which have been selected, copied, and deposited in this country. They were microfilmed for the author through the helpful services of the Department in Jackson. Hereafter referred to as "French Transcripts, Miss." See also Council of Marine to Cadillac and Duclos Paris, Feb. 15, 1716, Archives du Ministere des Colonies, Paris, B, Vol. 38, folio 287-88 vo. (The original had a map indicating the disposition of troops proposed by the Council, but the map cannot be located). Hereafter referred to as "Paris," this document and many others used in this work were microfilmed through the courtesy of the French officials and forwarded to the author; they will hereafter be referred to as "Paris." The Library of Congress now has copies of most of the manuscript documents used in this history.

²²Bienville to the Regency Council, May 10, 1717, *Miss. Prov. Arch., Fr. Dom.,* III, 221.

²³L'Epinay and Hubert to the Council, May 30, 1717, French Transcripts, Miss., AC., C 13, 5:27-31.

²⁴Cadillac to Pontchartrain, Feb. 2, 1716, *Miss. Prov. Arch., Fr. Dom.,* III, 201-02.

²⁵See the Council of Marine's decision to order the raising of the suspension of the officer (who was related to Bienville by Marriage) in Minutes of the Council, Sept. 8, 1716, Paris, AC., C 13, 4:323-24 vo. Cadillac charged that La Tour insulted him and, when the Governor sought to have him put under house arrest and surrender his sword, that La Tour had resisted. The latter charged Cadillac with refusing to allow him to submit a statement by other officers which would justify his conduct. *Ibid.,* Oc. 10, AM., B 1, 9:444.

III. THE CONSTRUCTION OF FORT TOULOUSE IN 1717.

[1]Crane, *Southern Frontier*, 256.

[2]Penicaut, *Annals of Louisiana from 1698-1722*, p. 127. Reynolds cites several sources for the description in his "Alabama-Tombigbee Basin," p. 90.

[3]Bienville and Salmon to Maurepas, Apr. 8, 1734, *Miss. Prov. Arch., Fr. Dom.,* III, 665.

[4]*Ibid.,* II, 209n.

[5]Giraud, *Historie de la Louisiane franciase*, II, 5-7, 38-40, 47-51 and *passim,* discusses his service.

[6]Pickett's account of the construction is found on pp. 192-96.

[7]*La Louisiane sous la Compagnie des Indes*, 1717-31, p. lxxviii.

[8]In two more detailed accounts which were unpublished, the proper date was given. These were "The Alabama-Tombigbee Basin in International Relations, 1701-1763," a Ph. D. thesis by Alfred W. Reynolds at the University of California, 1928, and the author's master's thesis, "Fort Toulouse and Its Subsequent History," pp. 9-11, written at the University of Alabama in 1928-29.

[9]A memorandum, probably dated 1713, French Transcripts, LC, AC., C 13c, 1:359 vo; l'Epinay and Hubert to the Council, May 30, 1717, French Transcripts, Miss., AC., C 13, 5:29-31 vo. There was a shortage of armorers as a rule, and Giraud indicated that one was not sent with the Alabama expedition (*Histoire de la Louisiane francaise*, II, 153).

[10]Description of Louisiana, N. d., [1704?], Paris, AC., C 13C 1:136 vo.

[11]Crane, *Southern Frontier*, p. 256-57.

[12]Hubert to the Council of Marine, Oct. 26, 1717, *Miss. Prov. Arch., Fr. Dom.,* II, 250. See also Bienville to Hubert, Sept. 19, 1717, *ibid.,* III, 222-23. The traders asked to be recompensed for the loss of their goods and La Tour supported their request (*Ibid;* Guenot de Trefontain to l'Epinay, Oct. 2, 1717, French Transcripts, Miss., AC., C 13, 5:119).

[13]Crane, *Southern Frontier*, p. 256; La Tour to Hubert, Fort Toulouse, Mch. 17, 1718, French Transcripts, Miss., AC., C 13, 5:117-18 vo.

[14]Bienville to Hubert, Sept. 9, *Miss. Prov. Arch., Fr. Dom.,* III, 222-23.

[15]Crane, *Southern Frontier*, p. 256-57.

IV. ITS MILITARY ROLE AND HISTORY TO 1750

[1]Villiers du Terrage, *Les dernieres annees de la Louisiane francaise* (Paris, 1904), pp. 109-10.

[2]An example is in the Memoir on Louisiana probably by Bienville in 1726, *Miss. Prov. Arch., Fr. Dominion,* III, 512.

[3]Reynolds, "Alabama-Tombigbee Basin, " p. 99.

[4]Regulations on the Administration of Affairs of the Colony of Louisiana, Sept. 5, 1721, French Transcripts, LC, AC., B 43:26-29.

[5]Descloseaux to the Minister, Oct. 25, 1748, French Transcripts, Miss., AC., C 13, 32:222ff. There appears to have been at least one conspiracy against the French by other Creeks—the Abikhas and Cowetas—which was apparently disclosed by the Chaounons. Maurepas to Vaudreuil, Feb. 14, 1749, French Manuscripts, LC, AC., B 89:35vo.

[6]Memoir on Louisiana, apparently by Bienville in 1726, Miss. Prov. Arch., Fr. Dom., III, 508-16.

[7]Bienville to Maurepas, New Orleans, Sept. 30, 1734, ibid., I 243.

[8]Crane, Southern Frontier, p. 261.   [9]Ibid., 191.

[10]Peter A. Brannon, The Southern Indian Trade (Montgomery, Ala., 1935), p. 9.

[11]In 1721, for example, the Choctaws were at war with the unfriendly Chickasaws and the price paid by the French was a gun, a pound of powder, and two pounds of bullets for Chickasaw Indian scalps and eighty livres for a slave. (Extract from the Register of the Minutes of the Council, Feb. 8, Miss. Prov. Arch., Fr. Dom., III, 375.) Two later, other Indians were induced to make war on the Natchez, who had become anti-French, by offering the same compensation. (Sept. 16, and 18, 1723, ibid., 374-77.) Apparently, this was after these Indians had murdered two Frenchmen and when French forces had marched against them, burned two villages, and had had "twelve heads of the assassins" brought in. (Memoir on the Services of Bienville, 1725, ibid., 493,) Bienville tells of having brought to him the heads of two prominent Choctaw chiefs who had travelled "to Carolina to invite the English to come and settle among them." (Ibid., 490-91)

[12]Crane, Southern Frontier, pp. 185-86.

[13]Minutes of the Superior Council of Louisiana, May 28, 1723, Miss. Prov. Arch., Fr. Dom., III, 348-49. One consideration had been higher pay for service at this base to make up for the shortage of food, etc., but the disorders continued.

[14]Pickett, History of Alabama, pp. 229-30.

[15]La Harpe, Journal historique, p. 261, differs with Pickett as to detail as does Charles Gayarre, History of Louisiana, French Domination, Vol. 1 (New York, 1850).

[16]It was reported to be twenty-five in 1718, according to Bobee to de l'Lisle, Mobile or Dauphin Island, Sept. 20, 1718, French Transcripts, LC, Box 1409, Archives Service Hydrographiques (hereafter referred to as ASH), Vol. 115xvi, No. 4. According to this account, the same number were at Natchez and Natchitoches, twice as many were at New Orleans, and there was none at Illinois. What would appear to be an accurate statement was made by Diron to the Minister Mobile, Dec. 9, 1728, AC., C 13, 11:176vo, in which he said there were 22 men, 2 corporals, 1 sergeant, and 2 officers—a total of 27. He said 100 were needed. The size was reported to be only nineteen a little later (1 lieutenant,

a sergeant, a corporal, and 16 fusiliers) as given in a list of Troops at Different Posts, New Orleans, n.d., but probably 1731, French Transcripts, LC, AC., D 2c, 50:7. This gives only a garrison of 38 for Mobile, 33 for Balize, 13 for Natchitosis, but 93 for Natchez. Beauchamp's Report of an Inspection of Garrisons, at Mobile, the Alabamas, and Dauphin Island on Nov. 6, 1731, Paris, AC., C 13a, 13:202, gave a total force of two companies, 84 men, for the three posts. This is probably more accurate than the figure of 60 troops at the Alabama fort during its early history as found in an Extract from Deliberations, Service Historique de l'Armee a Vincennes, Correspondence, Vol. 1, 2592, fo. 149vo-51. The same source, however, gives the garrison as 58 soldiers, 3 officers, a clerk, and a surgeon in 1720, (Ibid., A¹, Vol. 2592, fo. 89 vo.)

[17]Bienville to the Council of Marine, Dec. 15, 1721, Miss. Prov. Arch., Fr. Dom., III, 316-17; Minutes of the Superior Council of Louisiana, May 28, 1723, ibid., 348-349. The first report on the mutiny was by Bienville to the Council of Marine, Sept. 25 and further details are probably in this communication.

[18]In the Distribution of Troops, Paris, Sept. 23, 1724, Paris, AC., B 43:459, a Sub-Lieutenant Hersant, one of his subordinates, was then detached and serving at the Alabamas. In the Minutes of the Superior Council of May 20, 1724, Miss. Prov. Arch., Fr. Dom., III, 400, he is shown to have joined with two other officers who were familiar with the Alabama garrison to recommend a raise in the pay of a soldier who had served as master of the boat at the post. His company was still stationed at Fort Conde (Mobile) in 1731 when Lieutenant Benoist, one of his subordinates, was stationed at Fort Toulouse. A Review of the Garrison there, for November, 1731, Paris, AC., C 13a, 13:202.) There are other references to his service in this period.

[19]Father Raphael to Abbet Raquet, New Orleans, May 15, 1725, Miss. Prov. Arch., Fr. Dom., II, 483.

[20]Bienville to the Minister, June 12, 1737, AC., C 13a, 22:91 vo.

[21]Memoir of the King to Serve as Instructions for Bienville (when he was returned to Louisiana as governor), Feb. 2, 1732, Miss. Prov. Arch., Fr. Dom., III, 548-49.

[22]Bienville to the Minister, June 12, 1737, Paris, AC., C 13a, 22:92vo.

[23]Perier to Diron, Aug. 22, 1729, French Transcripts, Miss., AC., C 13, 12:159 ff.

[24]Diron to Perier, Sept. 7, 1729, Páris, AC., C 13, 12:166. He was sending Ensign de Bonnille to the post as ordered.

[25]Bienville to Maurepas, May 18, 1733, Miss. Prov. Arch., Fr. Dom., III, 614.

[26]Captain Francois de Mandeville, Sieur de Marigny, was in command early in its history (Ibid., II, 29n), probably after La Tour's term. He returned to France and received the coveted Order of St. Louis and was back in the colony by 1721. He served at increasingly important posts until his death in 1728. He and his son, a Creole, both had testimonials of good conduct and efficient service by Bienville. N. M. Miller Surrey, Calendar of Manuscrips in Paris Archives and Libraries Relating to the History of the Mississippi Valley to 1803 [Carnegie

Institution, 1928], II, 1012). Diron d'Artaguiette, an officer who was to carve a distinguished though eventually tragic career in Louisiana, is said to have been there in 1724, many years before he was burned at the stake by the Chickasaws. (*Miss. Prov. Arch., Fr. Dom.*, I, 17 n, 56-57n.) Sub-Lieutenant Hersant may have been in command in the same year, 1724; at least he was serving there at that time. (Distribution of Troops, Paris, Sept. 23, 1724, Paris, AC., B 43:451.) Sieur Pechon may have once been in command. He became "Commandant and Major of the Alabamas," the supervisory post in Mobile. He appears to have been on a mission there at the time of his death in 1736. (Hamilton, *Colonial Mobile*, p. 192.) Lieutenant Terisse was there in 1727 when he was involved in a major quarrel with Pechon. (Perier to the Minister, Apr. 30, 1727, French Transcripts, Miss. AC., C 13, 10:217-17vo.)

Lieutenant Montmarguet was apparently there in 1730 and 1731. (List of officers and Commandants of Posts, Aug. 19, 1732, AC.. D2c, 50:30-33; n.d., but probably 1731, *ibid;* 50:7.)

Benoit or Benoist appears to have succeeded him; he was in command in 1731 and must have remained until 1734 or early 1735. (Review of the Garrison, Nov. 1731, Paris, AC., 13a, 13:202; letter to Perier, March 29, 1732, French Transcripts, Miss., AC., C 13, 14:12; Bienville to Maurepas, Apr. 30, 1735, *Miss. Prov. Arch., Fr. Dom.*, I, 260-61.)

Chevalier d'Erneville is known to have been in command in the winter of 1736-37. (Bienville to Maurepas, Abstract for the King, Feb. 28, 1737, *ibid.,* III, 696; Diron to Maurepas, May 8, 1737, *ibid.,* I, 341.)

Lieutenant Hazeur appears to have served two terms. He was there in 1738-39 (Bienville to Maurepas, Mch. 25, 1739, *ibid.,* III, 727), then he is reported as having replaced d'Erneville in 1742 (Surrey, *Calendar.,* II, 976-77), and being there early in 1743 (*Miss. Prov. Arch., Fr. Dom.,* III, 779-80), and 1744 (see f.n. 18 of section V of this paper.

Captain Le Sueur was in charge in 1748. (Descloseaux to the Minister, Oct. 25, 1748, French Transcripts, Miss., AC., C 13, 32:222-32.) He was rated a man of talent and of zeal for the service; he was especially capable in dealing with Indians, understanding their languages "perfectly". (Annotated List of Officers of Louisiana, probably 1746, French Transcripts, LC, AC., D2c, 51:190vo.)

Chevalier Montaut de Montberaut was in command as Captain in 1756-57. He came from a distinguished family and would remain in the Mobile area after Louisiana was ceded to England. Milo B. Howard has a biography of the Chevalier in manuscript form, a masters thesis in Auburn University Library. His signature is found on the Extract of Review of the French Garrison at the Alabamas, Jan. 1, 1756, *ibid.,* 51 n.p. and the Pay of the Company, Alabamas, 1757, *ibid.* In an Annotated List of Officers of Louisiana, (1746, French Transcripts, LC, AC., D2c, 51:89), he was rated as "very exact in all his duties, fulfilling them with zeal and goodwill," and as "capable of detail," and "most regular" in his conduct.

Jean Bossu, who visited the fort in 1759, says that Aubert succeeded Montberaut in that year. (*Noveaux voyages aux Indies occidentales* [2 vols., Paris, 1768], letters XIV, XV.)

Apparently, Capt. de Grandmaison was there in 1760 and 1761. (Return of Troops at Fort Toulouse, Mch. 1, 1760, *ibid.*, 52:317; June 1, 1761, *ibid.*, 52 n.p)

Lieutenant de Lanoue, also spelled Le Nouie, was in command thereafter. (Extract from the Review, Month of June, 1761, *ibid.*; Return of Troops at Fort Toulouse Garrison, Feb. 1, 1763, Paris, AC., C 11a, 99:433-36.)

[27]Surrey, *Calendar*, I, p. 375.

[28]Minutes of the Superior Council, May 20, 1723, *Miss. Prov. Arch., Fr. Dom.*, III, 346.

[29]Pauger to the Council of the Indies, New Orleans, May 29, 1724, French Transcripts, Miss., AC., C 13c, 8:57; same to Directors of the Company, Mobile, Mch. 23, 1725, *ibid.*, 13, 9:371vo - 72.

[30]Bienville and Salmon to Maurepas, Apr. 8, 1734, *Miss., Prov. Arch, Fr. Dom.*, III, 665; Minister to Bienville and Salmon, Oct. 3, 1736, French Transcripts, LC., AC., B 64:508. The Arkansas post was too small for a stockade enclosure, having only a dozen men, but the new buildings there consisted of: "A wooden house on sleepers thirty-two feet long by eighteen feet wide, roofed with bark, consisting of three rooms on the ground floor, one of which has a fireplace, the floors and ceilings of cypress, a powder magazine built of wood on sleepers ten feet long by eight feet wide, a prison built of posts driven into the ground, roofed with bark, ten feet long by eight feet wide, and a building which serves as a barracks, also of posts driven into the ground, forty feet long by sixteen feet wide, roofed with bark." (*Ibid.*). Since the size of the structures at the Alabama post is not known at this time, some indication might be had from this description of buildings in a lesser post.

[31]Descloseux to the Minister, Oct. 25, 1748, French Transcripts, Miss., Ac., C 13, 32:224-30; Surrey, *Calendar*, II, 1114.

[32]The attrition of the river bank at this point has continued, but the river does not appear to have washed away much of what is believed to have been the sites. Perhaps the exact locations of the fort must await further archaeological research.

[33]King to Bienville, Feb. 2, 1732, *Miss. Prov. Arch., Fr. Dom.*, III, 564. By comparison, the much larger garrison at Mobile had forty-one cannons, one cast-iron and seven iron mortars, and nine small mortars. Natchez had three cannons, three cast-iron and six iron mortars, and one cast-iron mortar-breech. The list indicated that the latter had additional lesser armament. For some reason, the number of cannon balls at the Alabama fort, if there were any, was not listed, whereas the number was given at the other four posts inventoried in the document. In his *Travels*, p. 355, Bartram says he saw "a few pieces of ordnance, four and six pounders."

[34]Memoir on Louisiana, someone has dated this as probably 1739, but it is more likely to have been 1729 or 1730, Paris, AE., Mem. et Docs., France, 1991: 92vo-100.

[35]Bienville to Maurepas, Apr. 14, 1735, *Miss. Prov. Arch., Fr. Dom.*, I, 258. Lieutenant Hazeur drove out an English trader in 1738, but he soon returned. (*Ibid.*, 415.)

[36]McDowell, *Journals of the Commissioners of the Indian Trade*, 1710-1718, p. 295, 309.

[37]*History of the American Indians*, p. 260.

[38]To William Pinckney, Dec. 18, 1751, William L. McDowell, Jr., ed., *Documents relating to Indian Affairs*, May 21, 1750-August 7, 1754, in *The Colonial Records of South Carolina* series (Columbia, 1958), p. 216.

[39]Bienville to Maurepas, Apr. 30, 1735, *Miss. Prov. Arch., Fr. Dom.*, I, 263; Maurepas to Bienville, Oct. 4, 1735, French Transcripts, LC., Oct. 4, 1735, AC., B 63:610.

[40]Norman W. Caldwell, "The Southern Frontier during King George's War," *Journal of Southern History*, VII (1941), 47-49.

[41]Glen to Duke of Bedford, Feb. 3, 1747-48, English Transcripts, LC, PRO, C. O. 5, Vol. 13, p. 239-43. His estimate of the size of the garrison at Fort Toulouse was correct—something under fifty men. He believed that the Swiss mercenaries would go over to the enemy rather than fight, that they felt they were forever banished.

V. LIFE ON THE POST

[1]The boats also brought pay for the garrison, but this was in the form of commodities, as will be shown.

[2]L'Epinay and Hubert to the Council, May 30, 1717, French Transcripts, Miss. AC., C 13, 5:28-31.

[3]N. M. Miller Surrey, *The Commerce of Louisiana during the French Regime* (New York, 1916), pp. 67-68, 74-76. In Diron to Maurepas, May 8, 1737, *Miss. Prov. Arch., Fr. Dom.*, I, 338-42, some of the boats are described, and one with fifteen oarsmen was being sent to the Alabamas the next day.

[4]Minutes of the Administrative Council, May 29, 1724, *ibid.*, III, 400. A *pot* at that time appears to have contained 2 French *pintes* or about three and a quarter U. S. pints. This would be a total of approximately sixty pints of brandy which he received a year. It was common practice for soldiers who were used as oarsmen to receive some extra pay.

[5]Letter from Giraud to the author, Nov. 15, 1959. See his *Historie de la Louisiane francaise*, II, 58-59 for description of the elaborate uniforms adopted for sergeants, drummers, and privates and p. 123, n. 3, for officers. One proposal was that the uniforms of Louisiana should be white, since this color had always been respected by savage nations. (Memoir on Louisiana, n.d. [1720?], French Transcripts, LC, AC., C 13c:290.)

[6]Bienville to Maurepas, May 18, 1733, *Miss. Prov. Arch., French Dom.*, III, 621.

[7]The authorities had a member of the garrison executed in 1740 for the murder of a native and Captain d'Erneville insisted that a red man be executed for killing a member of the garrison. (Hamilton, *Colonial Mobile*, p. 193.)

[8]In 1737 "Captain de Pacana, the great war chief" of the nearest village first exacted of the commander, d'Erneville, a promise that deserters would not be harmed before he agreed to track them down and return them. (Diron to Maurepas, May 8, 1737, *Miss. Prov. Arch., Fr. Dom.,* I, 340-41). The council of war at the fort respected the promise, "subject to the King's good pleasure." In the same case — or perhaps on a few months earlier, the record is not clear — five deserted, but only two were brought in by the natives. They were sent to Mobile and Bienville urged the Minister to respect the promise. (Feb. 28, 1737, *ibid.,* III, 697.)

[9]A map of about 1756 (Atlas in Bibliotheque du Depot des Cartes de la Marine, 13, rue de l'Universite, No. 4044 C, 55), shows these clearly. A photostated copy is in the William L. Clements Library. The word Pacana in French means black walnut and there is still a row of such trees on this spot. It had sixty men of fighting age and Tomopa had ninety according to this map. There were 380 men ascribed to the five or six villages of the Alabamas. An undated but carefully drawn map (Bibliotheque Nationale, Departement des Cartes, Ge DD 2987 [Collection d'Anville No. 8816] sent by Diron) gives the name of Pacana to both, with Tomopa located across the Coosa and well above the post.

[10]Census of the Inhabitants of Toulouse Fort, n.d., an annex of Kerlerec to the Minister, Dec. 12, 1758, Paris, AC., C 13A, 40:157-57vo. A document in the Ministry of War Archives dated in 1720 claimed that 10 women and 22 former soldiers had already settled there; the figures are probably as incorrect as another one which claimed that 61 officers and men were in the garrison at that early date. (Archives du Service historique de l'Armee a' Vincennes, A[I], 259 2:89vo). One apparently accurate report indicates that there were no inhabitants there in 1724 except four or five traders. (Recapitulation of General Census of Louisiana, Dec. 20, 1724, French Transcripts, LC, A C., G1, 465, n.p.) Some of the government records, especially those written in Paris, were very inaccurate. The directors of the Company claimed that about forty inhabitants were there by 1731, a figure which was probably too high. (Extract from Deliberations, n.d., Service Historique de l'Armee, Correspondance, Vol. 2592, fo. 149vo-150, 151). A "Description of Louisiana," apparently in 1740, indicates that no land was in cultivation at the time. (Paris, AC., C 13c, 1:136 vo.) A surgeon-deserter told the Georgia Council in 1755 that about 140 men, women, and children lived in and about the fort and 42 were in the garrison. (*Col. Records of State of Ga.,* VII, 134.) Governor Kerlerec reported to the Minister in 1758 that children of the inhabitants were reared among the savages. (Dec. 12, 1758, Paris, AC., C 13a, 40:153vo-154.)

[11]Church records in Mobile lists baptisms of children born in the area when a Jesuit was not stationed there. (Hamilton, *Colonial Mobile,* 192.)

[12]Decree of May 13, 1723, *Miss Prov. Arch., Fr. Dom.,* II, 289-90.

[13]Officers did not always have the opportunity to have this supplied to them. It was a privilege they wanted since they had to pay more when purchased on the free market. (Bienville to Maurepas, May 18, 1733, *ibid.,* III, 620.) At one time all officers were given the privilge of purchasing from the storehouse (today one would say PX) brandy and flour at reduced prices. (Minutes of the Superior Council, June 21, 1724, *ibid.,* 404.) Commanders of posts were given

privileges of buying wine, brandy, and bread in an earlier Council meeting. (Minutes of the Council of Commerce, April 25, 1719, *ibid.*, 241.)

[14]Ordinance of the Company, Nov. 7, 1718; French Transcripts, LC, AC., B 42bis:257-60.

[15]Minutes of the Superior Council of Louisiana, May 28, 1723, *Miss. Prov. Arch., Fr. Dom.*, III, 348-49.

[16]*Ibid.*, 324; Minutes of the Administrative Council, July 17, 1722, *ibid.*, 326. See also Surrey, Commerce of Louisiana, p. 162, which shows that in bulk the price was 10 sous for a gallon of wine and 20 for brandy.

[17]In 1718 powder was 1½ francs a pound. (Ordinance of the Company of the West, Nov. 7, 1718, Paris, AC., B 42bis:257-60.) By 1756 powder was a franc a pound and balls were 8 sous a pound. (Extract of Review of the French Garrison Existing *aux Alibamons*, Jan. 1, 1756, French Transcripts, LC, AC., D 2c 51:n.p.) A franc was 20 sous.

[18]See for example, Extract of the Review of the French Garrison at the Alabamas, Jan. 1, 1756, French Transcripts, LC, AC., D 2c, 51:n.p.

[19]Abstract of the Minutes of the Superior Council, Apr. 21, 1722, *Miss. Prov. Arch., Fr. Dom.*, II, 271.

[20]Minutes of the Council of Commerce, Mch. 12, 1719, *ibid.*, II, 237. At the same time, it was decided to send Sarrazin as the next clerk there (*Ibid.*, 238).

[21]Itemized Statement of Expenses of the Company, Oct. 18, 1728, French Transcripts, LC, AC., B 43:827-28, 831.

[22]List of Employees serving in Louisiana, 1733, ibid., D 2d, 10:n.p. He was still listed as serving in both capacities in 1744 at 600 livres per year, and the interpreter at the Alabamas in 1744, a man named Vasseur, was paid 450. He was one of 6 interpreters then on the payroll, soon to be increased to 7. (List of Missionaries, Religious, and Civil Employees, 1744, *ibid.*)

[23]Extract of the Review of the French Garrison Existing at the Alabamas, Jan. 1, 1756, *ibid.*, D 2c, 51:n.p.

[24]Extract from the Review of the Month of June, Alibamas, June 1, 1761, *ibid.*, 52:n.p.

[25]Bienville to Hubert, Sept. 19, 1717, *Miss Prov. Arch., Fr. Dom.*, III, 222-23.

[26]AC., C 13A, 5:66, 117, as given in a letter from Giraud to the author, Nov. 15, 1959.

[27]Minutes of the Council of Commerce, Mch. 12, 1719, French Transcripts, LC., AC., C 13a, 5:329.

[28]This particular list was "General Roll of Troops of Louisiana 1734-1771," *ibid.*, D² C, 54:n.p. This is an alphabetical list of some 1900 names in 144 pages. The great majority of those who lost their lives in one way or the other, or deserted, were not identified as to place. There must have been a number of members of the Alabama garrison who died while in service. This list gives only

Jacques Simon Brignac, on August 10, 1755 and Jean-Louis Fonteneau, October 29, 1755.

[29]Minutes of the Council of Commerce, Mch. 12, 1719, *Miss. Prov. Arch., Fr. Dom.*, III, 238.

[30]Minutes of the Superior Council, May 28, 1723, *ibid.*, 349.

[31]Surrey, *Commerce of Louisiana*, p. 170.

[32]Various Expenses, Alabamas, 1759, French Transcripts, LC., AC., D 2c, 52:169-70. In the same year, Antoine Bonin was given a 200 franc bonus for having baked bread *"des sauvages"* during the last seven months of the year. (Itemized Statement of Sums Paid, Fort Toulouse, Dec. 31, 1751, *ibid.*, p. 67.)

[33]Reynolds, "Alabama-Tombigbee Basin," p. 244.

[34] This was true on the coast in 1723, and there is no reason to think it was different at inland posts. (Minutes of the Superior Council, June 5, 1723, *Miss. Prov. Arch., Fr. Dom.*, III, 350-51.)

[35]Maurepas to Vaudreuil, Aug. 13, 1747, AC., B 85:231.

[36]Statement by Lantagnac, n. d., enclosure in Kerlerec to the Minister, Oct. 1, 1755, Paris, AC., C 13a, 39-40-44vo. See also same to same, Oct. 1, French Transcripts, Miss., AC., C 13, 39:37ff for the governor's proposal that he be permitted to continue in the service and at Fort Toulouse.

VI.   TRADE AT THE ALABAMA POST

[1]State of Florida, Pensacola, and Mobile, etc. in Col. Robertson to Major General Gage, Mch. 8, 1764, British Transcripts in the Library of Congress, Public Records Office, Colonial Office 5, Vol. 83, LC pagination 117. Hereafter cited as British Transcripts, LC, PRO, CO. 5.

[2]See for example Minister to Vaudreuil and Michel, Sept. 26, 1750, French Transcripts, LC, AC., B 91:391-91vo.

[3]Minutes of the Council of Commerce, May 24, 1720, *Miss. Prov. Arch., Fr. Dom.*, III, 289-90; Minutes of the Superior Council, Jan. 27, 1725, *ibid.*, 483; Memoir on Louisiana, apparently by Bienville, 1726, *ibid.*, 516-17.

[4]Bienville and Salmon to Maurepas, Apr. 5, 1734, *ibid.*, 651-52.

[5]Crane, *Southern Frontier*, map following p. 326.

[6]*Ibid.*, 126-28, 135.

[7]Surrey, *Commerce of Louisiana*, p. 89. The horses wore bells, the Indians whooped, and the drivers cursed their horses, so there was a "continuous uproar" as the trains moved along.

[8]*Ibid.*, 89-90. For a review of the trading paths, commodities traded, and traders see Brannon, *Southern Indian Trade*, which also contains numerous excellent illustrations.

⁹The Indian products at the fort in 1724 were described in "Condition of Infantry Companies . . . and Inhabitants," Dec. 20, 1724, French Transcripts, LC, AC., G 1, 465:n.p., as much *d'huile dource*, fowl, and deerskins . . ."

¹⁰Crane, *Southern Frontier*, p. 117.

¹¹Extract from the Review of the Month of June 1, 1761, French Transcripts, LC, AC., D 2c, 52:n.p.; same for Mch. 1762, *ibid*. As late as February 1763, the garrison was paid 86 pounds of powder, and 215 pounds of balls, although apparently there was not enough on hand to meet the full payroll and retain a sufficient reserve. These were the only commodities paid the men, whereas in earlier years they had been paid in various commodities. (Return of Troops, Alabamas, Feb. 1, 1763, ibid.) When the post was evacuated in 1763, there was more powder than could be shipped to Mobile in the boats available.

¹²Surrey, *Commerce of Louisiana*, pp. 358-59.

¹³Decres of the Superior Council, Mch. 29, 1727, Surrey, *Calendar*, I, 465; by order of the *ordonnateur*, 1734, Surrey, *Commerce of Louisiana*, pp. 275-76. See also Bienville and Salmon to Maurepas, June 10, 1737, *Miss. Prov. Arch., Fr. Dom.*, III, 698-99.

¹⁴Surrey, *Commerce of Louisiana*, pp. 358-59.

¹⁵Extract of the Review of the Garrison, Alabamas, Jan. 1, 1756, French Transcripts, LC, AC., D 2c, 51:n.p.; Return of the Troops Garrisoned at Alabamas, Mch. 1, 1760, *ibid.*, 317-18vo.

¹⁶Bienville reported a good profit on this cloth in 1737. See his report with Salmon to Maurepas, June 10, *Miss. Prov. Arch., Fr. Dom.*, III, 698-99.

¹⁷In Vaudreuil and Salmon to the Minister, July 21, 1743, French Transcripts, Miss., AC., C13, 28:24ff., the last five of these commodities are given as items traded there.

¹⁸Minister to Bienville, Oct. 6, 1741, French Transcripts, LC, AC., B 72: 480vo; Maurepas to Vaudreuil and Salmon, Oct. 22, 1742, *ibid.*, 74:654vo-55vo; Maurepas to Hazeur, Jan. 29, 1744, *ibid.*, 78:461; Minister to Vaudreuil, Oct. 25, 1747, *ibid.*, 85:247vo; Bienville and Salmon to Maurepas, Feb. 7, 1743, *Miss. Prov. Arch., Fr. Dom.*, III, 779-80; Vaudreuil and Salmon to Maurepas, July 21, 1743, French Transcripts, Miss., AC., C 13, 28:24ff.

¹⁹Regulations on the Administration of Affairs of the Colony, Sept. 5, 1721, French Transcripts, LC, AC., B 43:22; Surrey, *Commerce of Louisiana*, p. 252. This must not have continued to be the practice for in 1758 these Indians were reported to be continually asking for trade at the same price as the Choctaws. (Enclosure, Kerlerec to the Minister, apparently Dec. 12, 1758, French Transcripts, LC, AC., C 13a, 40:154.)

²⁰Bienville to Maurepas, Apr. 23, 1735, *Miss. Prov. Arch., Fr. Dom.* I, 261-63; summarized in Surrey, *Commerce of Louisiana*, pp. 354-55. The official rate Bienville and Salmon had set for pelts in the preceding spring was 25 sous per pound in exchange for goods at the commissary. (Bienville and Salmon to Maurepas, April 5, 1734, *Miss. Prov. Arch., Fr. Dom.*, III, 651-52.)

[21]Bienville and Salmon to Maurepas, Sept. 2, 1736, *Miss. Prov. Arch.*, *Fr. Dom.*, III, 690-91; same to same, Sept. 13, *ibid.*, 691-92.

[22]For example see: Minutes of the Superior Council of Louisiana, July 23, 1723, *ibid.*, 356, which read that "we never have enough merchandise, the English furthermore trade for their peltries at a rate far higher than that at which the French to receive them;" Diron to Maurepas, May 8, 1737, *ibid.*, I, 341; Vaudreuil to the Minister, Apr. 1, 1746, French Transcripts, Miss., AC., C 13, 30: 53-54; Surrey *Commerce of Louisiana*, pp. 358-59, 364-65; Vaudreuil and Salmon to the Minister, July 21, 1743, French Transcripts, Miss., AC., C 13, 28:24ff; Kerlerec to the Minister, Dec. 19, 1754, *ibid.*, 38:122-32vo.

[23]Colonial Chicken's Journal, August 21, 1725, as given in Mereness, *Travels in the American Colonies*, p. 129.

[24]McDowell, *Journals of the Commissioners of the Indian Trade*, 1710-1718, pp. 309-11.

[25]For example, if the rival traders showed a lack of consideration for their customers, Governor Vaudreuil didn't know it in 1743, when he described them as quite willing even to fraternize with their customers. (To the Minister, July 21, 1743, French Transcripts, Miss., AC., C 13, 28:24ff.) It is interesting to note that each of the rivals thought the traders of the other were more accommodating.

[26]Reynolds, "Alabama—Tombigbee Basin," p. 92; French, *Historical Collections of Louisiana*, II, 236.

[27]Crane, *Southern Frontier*, pp. 258n.

[28]Condition of the Infantry Companies . . . and the Inhabitants, Dec. 20, 1724, French Transcripts, LC, AC., G1, 465:n.p.

[29]*Miss. Prov. Arch.*, *Fr. Dom.*, III, 536-38. He lists 4 villages and 300 Alabama warriers, 6 Tallapoosa villages 4 leagues to the east with 600 men, and 11 Abikha towns 20 leagues to the north with 1000 men. He reported that the Tallapoosaand Abekas were neutral and would trade only with the French if goods were available.

[30]Statement of Finances, Jan., 1732 to Jan. 1, 1739. Paris AC., F3, 159:94.

[31]*Ibid.*, 96.

[32]Enclosure in Colonel Robertson's letter to Major General Gage, Mch. 8, 1764, British Transcripts, PRO, CO., 5, 83:117.

[33]Enclosure, Kerlerec to the Minister, Dec. 12, 1758, Paris, AC., C 13a, 40:154.

[34]Candler, *Colonial Records of Georgia*, VIII, *Journal*, 1759-1762, p. 524. A map drawn by the French about 1756 supports about the same conclusion. (Manuscript Map, Bibliotheque Nationale, Paris, MSS 4044 C, 55, which has been copied and deposited in the William L. Clements Library of the University of Michigan.)

[35]Louboey to Maurepas, Jan. 4, 1740, *Miss. Prov. Arch.*, *Fr. Dom.*, I, 415. This was when Hazeur had reported that a French trader he had driven out of

a neighboring village had returned, that since the post lacked "everything in general and brandy in particular," he could not force him out a second time. Louboey despatched at once a boatload of goods.

VII.   FORT TOULOUSE AS A MISSIONARY CENTER

[1]McDowell, *Documents relating to Indian Affairs, 1750 - 1754*, p. 216.

[2]*Miss. Prov. Arch., Fr. Dom.*, III, 515.

[3]State of the Church in Louisiana before the Introduction of the Jesuits into the Lower Part of the Colony, prob. 1728, *ibid.*, II, 569-72; John G. Shea, *The Catholic Church in Colonial Days* (New York, 1886), pp. 566-67.

[4]Estimate of the Missionary Priests who Fill the Posts of the Colony, 1724, French Transcripts, LC, AC., D 2d, 10:n.p., Estimate of the Priests, Missionaries, at the Posts, n.d., but the year 1725 appears in the document, French Transcripts, Miss., AC., C13, 10:72vo-73.

[5]Father Raphael To Abbot Raguet, May 15, 1725, *Miss. Prov. Arch., Fr. Dom.*, II, 483.

[6]Father Raphael to Abbot Raguet, May 15, 1725, *ibid.*, 470-92; Sept. 15, *ibid.*, 505-15; May 18, 1726, *ibid.*, 515-32. He pointed out how hard it was to exist on the allotment of 600 francs especially at posts such as the Alabamas where one could not expect altar fees of any consequence since there were so few communicants and these were so poor.

[7]Reuben G. Thwaites, ed., *The Jesuit Relations and Allied Documents* (Cleveland, 1900), LXXI, 169; *ibid.*, LXX, 229; John G. Shea, *History of the Catholic Missions among the Indian Tribes of the United States, 1529-1854* (New York 1855), p. 502.

[8]Statement of the Missionary Priests who Fill the Posts of Louisiana, Nov. 17, 1728, French Transcripts, LC, AC., D 2d, 10 n.p.

[9]Perier and la Chaise to the Directors of the Company, Jan. 30, 1729, *Miss. Prov. Arch., Fr. Dom.*, II, 611-12.

[10]Perier and la Chaise to the Directors, Sept. 6, 1729. *ibid.*, 643. Notes on the deliberation held about this were made and forwarded to the Directors, and the Company approved all that was done and wished the missionary success.

[11]Thwaites, *Jesuit Relations*, LXVIII, 221; Shea, *Catholic Missions*, 449. He was involved in some sort of controversy with M. Bru of Mobile; as a consequence, a copy of a letter he wrote (apparently from the Fort) is found in the Paris Archives, AC., C 13 a, 12:212.

[12]Letter by Vivier, Nov. 17, 1750, Thwaites, *Jesuit Relations*, LXIX, 205. Shea, *Catholic Missions*, p. 502, places him there in 1730 and indicates that he may have served for a time after that date. Shea in his *Catholic Church in Colonial Days* has him arriving at the Alabamas in 1735. It was probably during his stay that a cargo of goods destined for the mission was lost on the river, and

the Company was asked to make good the value to the amount of 800 francs. (Memoir on Jesuit Missions in Louisiana, 1732, Paris, AC., C2 25:93-94vo.)

[13]Royal Memoir to Serve as Instructions to Bienville, Sept. 2, 1732, French Transcripts, LC, AC., B 57:796vo.

[14]Shea, *The Catholic Church in Colonial Days*, p. 584.

[15]*Nouveaux voyages*, Letters XIV, XV.

[16]List of Jesuits Who Have Been on Mission in Louisiana Sept. 16, 1763, Paris, AC., D 2d, 10:n.p.

[17]*Southern Frontier*, p. 152.

[18]Reynolds, "Alabama and Tombigbee Basin," 216-17.

VIII. THE FORT AS A DIPLOMATIC CENTER

[1]To Hubert, Sept. 19, 1717, *Miss. Prov. Arch., Fr. Dom.*, III, 222-2223.

[2]Hubert to the Council, Oct. 26, 1717, *ibid.*, II, 250.

[3]Diron to the Minister, Dec. 9, 1728, French Transcripts, Miss., AC., C 13, 11:174-75 vo.

[4]Pauger to the Directors of the Company, Mch. 23, 1725, French Transcripts, Miss., AC., C 13, 9:371vo ff.

[5]Hubert to the Council, Oct. 26, 1717, *Miss. Prov. Arch., Fr. Dom.*, II, 250.

[6]Minutes of the Council of Commerce, Dauphine Island, Sept. 13, 1719, *ibid.*, III, 260.

[7]*Ibid.*, 260-61.

[8]Royal Memoir to Bienville and Salmon, Feb. 2, 1732, *ibid.*, 576.

[9]Bienville to Maurepas, Sept. 30, 1741, *ibid.*, III, 753.

[10]La Lande to Salmon, Dec. 14, 1740, Paris, AC., C 13a, 26:124-25vo. "Pow-wow" is not a bad term for the long and flowery speeches which were customary on such occasions. Actually, the contingent arrived too late for the meeting with the Choctaws at this time. Gifts had been distributed, however, and an effort was made to arrange a peace in case the Abikhas would be willing. The cessation of hostilities did not come easily even after the meeting. For the further efforts of the Alabamas, see Beauchamp to the Minister, Jan. 25, 1741, *ibid.*, 204 and Lou-boey to the Minister, Sept. 24, 1743, French Transcripts, Miss., AC., C 13, 28:160.

[11]Bossu, *Nouveaux voyages*, pp. 13-15; *Colonial Records of Georgia*, Vol. XVI.

[12]Fitch's Journal, Nov. 3-4, 1725, Mereness, *Travels in the American Colonies*, pp. 199-202. The victory was not altogether Fitch's. After he had Seepeycoffee's agreement to lead an expedition against the Yamasees, a negro from the fort over-took the force and persuaded about seventy warriors to turn back. (Crane, *Southern Frontier*, p. 268.)

[13]Mereness, *Travels in the American Colonies*, pp. 215-16.

[14]Bienville to Maurepas, May 8, 1740, *Miss. Prov. Arch., Fr. Dom.*, III, 732.

[15]McDowell, *Colonial Records of S. C., Documents relating to Indian Affairs*, 1750-54, pp. 4-5.

[16]P. 260.

[17]*Ibid.*, pp. 348-49.

[18]*Ibid.*, p. 322.

[19]Perier and La Chaise to the Directors, Mch. 25, 1729, *Miss. Prov. Arch., Fr. Dom.*, II, 639.

[20]Verner W. Crane, "A Lost Utopia of the First American Frontier," *The Sewanee Review*, XXVII (1919), 48-61; Journal of Antoine Bonnefoy, 1741-1742, *Mereness Travels in the American Colonies*, p. 249.

[21]Kerlerec to the Minister, Apr. 1, 1756, Paris, AC., C 13a, 39: 146-49vo; Minister to Berryer, July 28, 1756.

[22]Bienville to Maurepas, Mch. 15, 1734, *Miss Prov. Arch., Fr. Dom.*, III, 635.

[23]Mereness, *Travels in the American Colonies*, pp. 249-50; 255.

[24]Salmon to Maurepas, Oct. 4, 1741, *Miss Prov. Arch., Fr. Dom.*, III, 757.

[25]Copy of a letter by Benoist, probably to Perier, Mch. 29, 1732, French Transcripts, Miss., AC., C 13 14:12-13 vo. See also Kerlerec to the Minister, Oct. 9, 1755, Surrey, *Calendar*, II, 1284.

[26]Bienville to Maurepas, Feb. 28, 1737, *Miss. Prov. Arch., Fr. Dom.*, III, 696-97.

[27]Bienville to Maurepas, Mch. 25, 1739, *ibid.*, 727-28. Other reports of a somewhat similar nature are found in Bienville to the Minister, Sept. 20, 1741, Paris, AC., C 13a, 26:111-11vo., and same to same, Feb. 18, 1742, *Miss. Prov. Arch., Fr. Dom.*, III, p. 759.

[28]Kerlerec to the Minister, Oct. 10, 1755, French Transcripts, Miss., AC., C 13, 39:63-65.

[29]As an illustration, when d'Erneville heard of a Cherokee intention to invade Choctaw territory, he reported it to LeSueur, who was then in command at Tombecbe and would later be sent to the Alabama post. (Apparently 1740, Paris, AC., C 11, 114:135ff.)

[30]Bienville to Maurepas, Apr. 14, *Miss. Prov. Arch., Fr. Dom.*, I, 258.

[31]Bibliotheque Nationale, Paris, MSS 4044 C, 55, which has been copied and deposited in the William L. Clements Library.

[32]Candler, *Colonial Reocrds of Georgia*, VIII, *Journal*, 1759-62, 524. The French map mentioned above gave the Alabama villages as: Pakana, just to the south of the fort; Tomopa, just to the east-southeast, with both of these nearby villages located on the Tallapoosa; a small village across the Coosa and a short

distance upstream called Okchayia; about four miles below the fort and again on the opposite bank, Tastiqui — no doubt Tuskegee; Conchatis, another three miles downstream and on the west bank of the Alabama; Chaouanons, a new village to the south of the latter but on the east bank; and Colome on the south bank of the Tallapoosa, east-southeast of the post. The British list gave John Rae as the English trader at "Oakchoys opposite the said fort" where there were 35 hunters and William Trewin as trader at Little Oakchoys with only 20 hunters. It listed these villages as having no English traders in 1761: "Welonkees, including red Ground," 70 hunters; "Puckanaw" — no doubt Pacana — with 30; "Tuskegee including Soosaw old Town," 40; and "Soosawtee including Tomhetaws" which was "close to the Barracks," 125 hunters.

[33]Bienville to Maurepas, Mch. 7, 1741, *Miss. Prov. Arch.*, *Fr. Dom.*, III, 743 Surrey reaches this conclusion in *Commerce*, p. 357.

[34]Vaudreuil to Minister, Dec. 28, 1744, Surrey, *Calendar*, II, 1036.

[35]Vaudreuil to the Minister, Mch. 15, 1747, French Transcripts, Miss., AC., C 13, 31:17ff.

[36]Vaudreuil to the Minister, Mch. 17, 1747, *ibid.*, 26ff.

[37]Vaudreuil to the Minister, May 10, 1751, *ibid.*, 35:102.

[38]To the Minister, June 1, 1756, AC., C 13, 39:170.

[39]This impression is gained from reading the records concerning the fort and Reynolds finds the 1749-53 period perhaps the most "promising of the entire French Regime, with the single exception of the 1715 period." (Alabama and Tombigbee Basin", pp. 301-02.)

[40]When reviewing the contest for the old southwest, Crane's conclusion is: "Only the excellence of the British trade counter - - balanced the superior position and diplomacy of the Spanish and French." (*Southern Frontier*, p. 115.)

[41]In a letter to the Upper Creeks, Governor Glen found the Lower Creeks unfriendly in 1752 (McDowell, *Documents relating to Indian Affairs*, 1750-54, p. 209), but in 1753 he made the sweeping claim that the Creeks, to the number of 2500 men, would support his cause. (To Lord Holderness, June 25, 1763, British Transcripts, LC, PRO., F.O. 5, 13:607.) He could not make good this claim.

IX. THE SHOW DOWN — THE FRENCH AND INDIAN WAR, 1754-63

[1]Kerlerec to the Minister, June 28, 1755, French Transcripts, Miss., AC., C 13, 39:23f.

[2]To William Pinckney, written in the Upper Creek country, Dec. 18, 1751, McDowell, *Documents relating to Indian Affairs*, 1750-54, p. 216.

[3]Soldiers at Various Posts, Sept. 10, 1754, French Transcripts, Miss., AC., C 13, 38:213.

[4]Extract of the Review of the French Garrison at the Alabamas, Jan. 1, 1756,

French Transcripts, LC. AC., D 2c, 51:n.p.; Mch. 1, 1760, *ibid.*, 52:317-18vo; Feb. 1, 1763, Paris, AC., D 2c, 52:n.p. and also cited as AC., C 11a, 99:433-36vo.

[5]Minister to Kerlerec, Jan. 26, 1756, French Transcripts, LC. AC. B 103:203.

[6]He expressed fear of a mutiny at the Alabama and Tombecbe posts which had given out of flour and even of corn in autumn of 1758. There was still a supply of flour in New Orleans, but Ordonnateur Richemore would not release it. (Kerlerec to Accaron, Oct. 4, 1758, *ibid.*, C 13, 40-93.) Rochemore's solution was the abandonment of the two posts. (Rochemore to the Minister, Mch. 6, 1759, Paris, AC., C 13, 41:184ff.) This feud was one of the bitterest in the long list of quarrels between governors and *ordonnateurs*.

[7]Kerlerec to the Minister, July 22, 1756, French Transcripts, Miss., AC., C 13, 39:181ff. The British did build Fort Loudon on the Tennessee in 1757.

[8]Candler, *Colonial Records of Georgia*, XVI, 147-49.

[9]*Ibid.*, 147-49, 161-64.

[10]Lyttleton to Admiral Boscowen, Aug. 22, 1758, English Transcripts, LC, PRO., C. O., 5, 18:1070-74.

[11]Same to same, Sept. 8, 1758, *ibid.*, 1077-79. It is interesting to note that the French on their side also had a plan of campaign against the English. This is indicated in Surrey, *Calendar*, II, 1332. The document, 14 pages in length, is listed as Kerlerec to the Minister, Nov. 25, 1758, Paris, AC., C 13, 40:99; 104.

[12]Lyttleton to Admiral Boscowen, Aug. 22, 1758, British Transcripts, LC. PRO., C. O., 5, 18:1070-74.

[13]Atkin to William Pitt, Mch. 27, 1760, *ibid.*, 64:245-46. See also Emile Lauvriere, *Histoire de la Louisiane francaise, 1673-1939* (Baton Rouge, 1940), p. 389, and Kerlerec to the Minister, June 12, 1759, cited in Marc de Villiers du Terrage, *Les dernieres annees de la Louisiane froncaise.* (Paris, 1903), pp. 107-08. In the latter report the governor gave credit to some of the Coweta and Alabama chiefs for the anti-English campaign, although he no doubt had an exaggerated idea of it.

[14]Atkin to Pitt, Mch. 27, 1760, British Transcripts LC, PRO., C. O. 5, 54:245-54.

[15]*Ibid.*, 250-51

[16]*Ibid.*, 267-69.

[17]The date is mistakenly given as 1716, "being the year after the breaking out of the Indian War with Carolina . . ."

[18]Oct. 10, 1759, British Transcripts, LC, PRO., C.O., 5, 64:273-79.

[19]Atkin to William Pitt, Mch. 27, 1760, *ibid.*, 253-54.

[20]Kerlerec to the Minister, June 24, 1760, Villiers du Terrage, *Les dernieres annes de la Louisiane*, pp. 109-10.

[21]Kerlerec to the Minister, July 25, 1760, Surrey, *Calendar*, II, 1379.

[22]Same to Same, Aug. 4, *Ibid.*, 1380.

[23]Bull to Amherst, Oct. 19, 1760, British Transcripts, LC, PRO., C. O. 5, 60:87-102.

[24]Statement of Dec. 31, 1760, French Transcripts, LC, AC., D 2c, 50:83f. Develle was rewarded much more than La Nove.

[25]To the Minister, Aug. 6, 1760, Surrey, *Calendar*, II, 1380. The harrassed man had good reason to suspect that the crown had indeed abandoned Louisiana; yet in July the minister of foreign affairs rejected flatly a Spanish suggestion that the two states might agree on an exchange of Spanish territory for the colony of Louisiana. (Surrey, *Calendar*, II, 1379.)

[26]Proceedings of the Council of War, Feb. 9, 1761, French Transcripts, LC, AC., F 3, 25:154-57vo.

[27]Herbert E. Bolton and Thomas M. Marshall, *The Colonization of North America*, 1492-1783 (New York, 1936), pp. 378-79 gives the figure of 1200 in 1790 and 2600 the next year.

[28]Boone, to Amherst, June 25, 1762, British Transcripts, LC, PRO., C. O. 5, 62:307.

[29]E. Wilson Lyon, *Louisiana in French Diplomacy* 1759-1804 (Norman, Oklahoma, 1934), pp. 15-17.

X. THE FORT IN THE TREATY NEGOTIATIONS

[1]Memoir, July 15, 1761, Archives du Ministere des Affaires Etrangeres, Correspondance Politique, Etats-Unis, Sup. 6, 79. Hereafter referred to as "AE., Cor. Pol."

[2]Bussy to the Minister, July 26, 1761, *ibid.*, Angleterre, 444:59.

[3]Surrey, *Calendar*, II, 1395.

[4]Additional Manuscripts, British Museum, No. 35421, fo. 83-84, LC pagination, 30-32; Stanley's response to French Communication of August 10, Sept. 1, 1761, AE., Cor. Pol., Angleterre, 444:233.

[5]Choiseul to Ossun, Oct. 9, 1762, Surrey, *Calendar*, II, 1431.

[6]Dec. 20, *ibid.*, 1434.

[7]Kerlerec to Minister, May 2, 1763, AC., French Transcripts, Miss., C 13, 43:196-96vo.

[8]Return of Troops, Alabamas, Feb. 1, 1763, Paris, AC., C 11A, 99:433-36 vo.

[9]Census of the Inhabitants of the Toulouse Fort, n.d. annex of Kerlerec to the Minister, Dec. 12, 1758, Paris, AC., C 13a, 40:157-57vo. The names of heads of families are given with the number of sons and of daughters.

[10]Kerlerec to the Minister, May 2, 1763, AC., Miss., C 13, 43:196vo-98. The governor still could not accustom himself to the permanent loss of a colony which had not been taken by force. He suggested that presents to the natives be continued, so that "France would live in the minds of the Indian nations," and perhaps the colony might not be hard to recover.

XI. THE FRENCH EVACUATION IN 1763 AND THE BRITISH DECISION NOT TO GARRISON THE FORT

[1]Memoir to Serve as Instructions, Feb. 10, 1763, French Transcripts, LC, AC., B 116:571-71vo. He has a 66 page journal which gives his experiences during the evacuation. It is in AC., C 13, 43:249ff, and is said to be among the French Transcripts in Jackson, Miss.

[2]Kerlerec to the Minister, July 4, 1763, French Transcripts, Miss., AC., C 13, 43:206ff.

[3]D'Abbadie to Col. Robertson, Dec. 7, 1763, French Transcripts, Miss., AC., C 13, 43:245ff.

[4]D'Abbadie to Kerlerec, Nov. 6, 1763, French Transcripts, Miss., AC., C 13, 43:235-38.

[5]Circular letter to the Lieutenant Governor of Virginia, Governors of N. C., S. C., and Ga., and John Stuart, New York, May 4, 1763, British Transcripts, LC, PRO, C. O. 5, Vol. 63, LC pagination 75-76; to Governor Boone, June 15, ibid., p. 225.

[6]D'Abbadie to Kerlerec, date unknown, French Transcripts, LC, AC., C 13c, 1:275ff; Aubry to the Minister, Jan. 15, 1764, Paris, AC., C 13a, 44:133-33vo.

[7]The State of Florida, Pensacola, Mobile, etc., in Robertson to Major General Gage, Mch. 8, 1764, British Transcripts, LC, PRO, CO., 5, Vol. 83, LC pagination 135-36.

[8]D'Abbadie to Kerlerec, date Unknown, but internal evidence indicates it was late in 1763 or early in 1764, French Transcripts, LC, AC., C 13c, 1:275-76. See also the last muster rolls.

[9]D'Abbadie to Kerlerec, Nov. 6, French Transcripts, Miss., AC., C 13, 43: 235-37vo, makes it clear that orders had not yet been given to evacuate the fort.

[10]Aubry to the Minister, Jan. 15, 1764, Paris, AC., C 13a, 44:133-33vo.

XII. SEQUEL

[1]James Germany was sent to take possession of the fort for the British, but there was little of value there, and he soon spent most of his time in the home which he established on the present site of Montgomery. (Hamilton, Colonial Mobile, p. 222.)

[2]For a brief review of this period in the history of the site, see the author's thesis, "Fort Toulouse and Its Subsequent History," University of Alabama Library, chap. VI.

[3]Mr. Peter A. Brannon, Director of the Alabama Department of Archives and History, read this account of Fort Toulouse in manuscript form. From his wide knowledge of Alabama history, he has saved the printed version from various mistakes and the author is deeply appreciative.